Walk

It

Out

Published by Walk it Out Ministries

P.O. Box 902
Elkhart, Texas 75839
United States of America
www.walkitoutministries.com

ISBN 13: 978-1-62166-801-5

Endorsements

Ginger Brown was once deeply bound in addiction and all its accompanying darkness, destruction, guilt, and shame. I watched her "Walk It Out" and now she enjoys the full restoration of all that was lost and the fulfillment of all her life's most precious dreams and desires. Her life is a miracle – a testimony – and this story can be yours too. Ginger received revelation on how to walk out of addiction and it is her pleasure to share these insights with you. Her book, *Walk it Out,* will help and support you one day at a time as you engage in your journey of freedom. I highly recommend this book.

Dr. Patricia King
www.patriciaking.com

I have had the privilege of knowing Ginger for about 6 years.

She is amazing. Her story is amazing. I look at her and have read her story of how God set her free and healed her. It is so wonderful. I have watched as God healed her, restored her girls to her and brought her an amazing husband. Then to be a part of praying in her twins from the beginning – this is such a miracle. Be sure to read this book. It will help you and others.

Joan Hunter
Author/Evangelist
www.JoanHunter.org

I remember when Ginger wrote this book while under a powerful anointing. She was growing by leaps and bounds both spiritually and emotionally and was in prayer several hours a day. I watched Ginger go from the pit to the palace. She is truly a new creation in Christ. Literally, her life went from a mess to a miracle and to this day she walks in perpetual provision. Where the Spirit of the Lord is, there is freedom and Ginger knows how to WALK IT OUT. I will always call her Miss Miracle and we love her to the moon.

Paulette Reed
Itinerant Speaker/Author
www.paulettereed.com

Dedication

This book is dedicated to my daughters,
Chelsea, Cheyanne, & Cierra.
I love you all so much.
Thank you for your love and forgiveness.
I look forward to a lifetime of restored relationship
with each of you.

And to my mom, Beverly...
How I thank you for all the years of prayer,
and never giving up on me!
You are amazing and I love you.

Foreword

Ginger Cato has written a beautiful gift. She has walked out of addiction and mapped a trail for others to follow. I've watched as Ginger lives out the principles shared in these pages. She walks with grace and beauty, illuminated from within by a joy and peace that has been found by laying hold of truth and walking it out. She displays the redeeming and restorative power of being in relationship with a living God.

Along with a map, Ginger reveals your compass on this journey: Jesus. He is your truth, always pointing the way to Father God. With Him, you never walk alone and you can't get lost. Ginger clearly presents that only Jesus is able to break the shackles of bondage, and set your feet on a path of freedom. When it feels like you can't walk anymore, He is there to carry you, heal your heart and love you... always love you. Jesus is the One Who can take all the pieces and put them back together again, restoring a shattered soul.

Ginger has an obvious love of scripture and its revelation of God's heart. As you read, you will see that God's greatest desire is relationship with you. It is a free gift that brings freedom. You can't earn your way into God's heart; but you can let your arms down and receive what is already yours - His love. Because He loves us so wonderfully, our desire is to know Him more and to please Him. As we walk out this desire, He continues to lavish His love on us. What a wonderful cycle of love!

"Walk It Out" with God and you'll find that you will begin to run and then soar, as you experience His goodness in every area of your life. So, open your heart and lace up those shoes...there is a joyous journey ahead of you!

Dr. Michelle Burkett
Patricia King Ministries
WIMN Director

My Journey

By the grace of God, I have been set free from a 15-year drug addiction. I started smoking crack in 1994 a few months after I had gotten my nursing license. I was 19 years old with a two-year-old daughter, and I was very excited about my future.

Within a few months of starting this drug, I quit my job as a nurse and lost everything, including my daughter. I was on the streets doing whatever it took to get my drugs, no matter how dangerous or demeaning. I didn't care about myself or anyone else. All I cared about was the next high.

The next 15 years of my life were pure hell. Satan set out to destroy me and did everything in his power to do so. (Thank God I had a praying Mom!)

I was consistently in and out of jails and rehabs. I finally gave up on rehab, but I continued to go to jail over and over again. I ended up with 22 misdemeanor and three felony convictions. Not to mention all the times I was arrested for tickets. I know I was arrested altogether at least 50 times and I spent a total of about six years of my life in jail or prison.

I lived through numerous near death experiences on the streets. Many girls, I knew along the way, did lose their lives.

Once, I actually died on a shot of cocaine. By grace, the drug addicts that were with me were able to revive me with CPR and a little "Divine Intervention."

Along the way I had two more daughters, giving birth to one of them while incarcerated. I just couldn't seem to get it together, even for them. My family ended up raising my daughters for me.

I had given my heart to God as a child, so every time I went to jail I would run back to Him for comfort, but I never truly surrendered my will and my life to Him. So, every time I would get out of jail I would eventually, if not immediately, go back to the drugs.

I finally realized that I could not just give God little pieces of my life and expect to receive freedom from my addiction. I understood that in order for Him to bring me freedom, I was going to have to surrender my life to Him 100%. I also knew there would be many steps I would have to take to walk out my deliverance (freedom from addiction).

In September 2008, I rededicated my life to God. This time I laid it all down, holding nothing back. I was truly "sick and tired of being sick and tired" and I was very hungry for the restoration only God can bring.

I started seeking Him with all my heart and spending as much time as possible in daily prayer and reading the Bible. Step by step, God has been showing me how to walk out my deliverance.

I have taken full responsibility for my life and the poor choices I made. We cannot continue to blame others for our mistakes and expect to gain freedom. A "victim mentality" will only keep us trapped.

While I take responsibility for my past actions and their consequences, I have been able to forgive myself and leave all of my shame and guilt at the feet of Jesus. I have also forgiven everyone who has ever hurt me, just as my Father in heaven has forgiven me.

I have been clean for over two years, and God has already changed my life more than I ever thought possible. He is teaching me how to love others and myself in a way that is healthy and pure. He is also bringing full restoration in my relationships with my children and other family members.

I no longer have the desire to use drugs. Now my greatest desire is to serve God and honor Him in everything I do. He has put a great burden on my heart to help reach addicts who are still suffering with the good news that we can all have freedom from addiction in Christ Jesus.

I have entitled this book *Walk it Out,* because that is what we must do in our deliverance. Deliverance means to be set free. God can supernaturally set us free from addiction but we need to "walk out" our deliverance by spending time with God in prayer, reading His Word, and applying the commandments and godly principles we learn in our everyday lives. In this way, we will gain true freedom.

I am sharing Bible verses with you, that have brought me release in areas of addiction and every other area of bondage (slavery to sin) in my life. I've explained how each verse can be used to walk out your deliverance. There is also a prayer included with each section and a set of decrees for each week. Speaking the decrees out loud, each day, is a very powerful way to pray. The Bible says in Job 22:28, "Decree a thing and it shall be established."

I also encourage you to use the "My Walk" pages, at the end of each week, to journal your journey, reflections, and all that God shares with you as you *Walk It Out.*

You will notice that I do not talk about addiction on every page of the book. I only mention it a few times because I believe it is better to stay focused on the solution rather than the problem.

Addiction was only a symptom of our spiritual disease. In God we have found the cure!

UPDATE

It is now January of 2018 and I have been clean for over 9 years! *Walk it Out* was first published in 2010 and since then we have been able to get almost 7,000 books into different prisons and outside recovery groups so far. Prison letters pour in every week with testimonies and requests for more books.

I am so honored that God used me to write this book and touch so many lives as they are being delivered from addiction the same way I was back in 2008.

During the last 9 years, God has done more for me than I could have ever asked for or imagined. My relationship with my three grown up daughters is fully restored. He sent me an amazing husband in 2012 and we just celebrated our fifth wedding anniversary. Also, the biggest miracle of all is that we have twin babies – Cason and Chloe – that will be two years old next month. The story of how they were conceived is a whole other miraculous testimony by itself. I am now 43 years old and also have two grandchildren, including one older than my twins

I can't begin to explain the joy that I have in my life each day as I continue to Walk it Out. It hasn't all been easy. There will always be challenges, but with God all things are possible! I pray this book continues to help many others *Walk it Out* in their own journey to freedom.

My husband Brad and I with our miracle twins – 2016

My family fully restored – Here I am at a recent get-together with my four daughters and son

Walk it Out!

Your Journey begins . . .

Daily Decrees

1. Jesus Christ is my Lord and Savior!

2. I am a redeemed child of God!

3. God has an awesome plan for my future.

4. Jesus loves me and I am very precious to Him.

5. I will only speak positive words that bring life to my family and me.

6. I let go of all shame and guilt from my past because I have been forgiven.

7. I forgive myself for every wrong choice or mistake I ever made.

8. I choose to renew my mind each day by reading the Word of God and applying it in my life and actions.

9. When I am tempted, I will not sin. I will ask God for help and He will strengthen me!

10. I will stay prepared for attacks from Satan, my enemy, by praying and reading God's Word each day.

Jesus Saves!

*If you confess with your mouth, "Jesus is Lord," and believe in your heart
that God raised Him from the dead, you will be saved.*
Romans 10:9 (NIV)

Wow! Isn't that amazing? All we have to do is confess that Jesus is Lord and believe in His resurrection to receive eternal salvation!

By His death and resurrection, Jesus brings salvation to those who believe in Him. Salvation can be defined as deliverance from the guilt and power of sin. Jesus, who lived a life totally without sin, paid the price for our sin on the cross. He took all of our sin and the punishment we deserved upon Himself. Because of Jesus, we have forgiveness for all of our transgressions. Through His sacrifice, we are set free from the penalty of sin, which is death, and we are given eternal life instead!

*For God so loved the world that He gave His
only begotten Son, that whosoever believeth
in Him, should not perish
but have everlasting life.*
John 3:16

If you have not yet accepted Jesus as your Lord and Savior, what are you waiting for?

Accepting Jesus into your heart is the only way you can obtain true freedom in every area of your life. In Him, you can become free from addiction, depression, sickness and disease, unhealthy relationships, pain from your past, anxiety and worry, among other things that take away from your quality of life.

Ask Jesus to forgive you for your sins, and come into your heart now. It will be the best decision you ever made!

Prayer of Salvation

Father God, it is written in Your word that if I confess Jesus as Lord and believe in my heart You raised Him from the dead, I shall be saved. Right now, I confess that Jesus is my Lord. I choose to make Him Lord of my life. I also believe in my heart that You raised Him from the dead. I thank You for forgiving me of all my sins. Thank You for my eternal salvation and freedom in Jesus Christ. In Jesus' Name I pray, Amen.

Reflection

In what areas of my life would I like to receive freedom?

Scripture Reading

John 3 & Romans 6:23

Rescued

The Spirit of the Lord is upon me, because He hath anointed me to preach the gospel to the poor; He hath sent me to heal the brokenhearted, to preach deliverance to the captives, and recovering of sight to the blind, to set at liberty them that are bruised.
Luke 4:18

Every human being is created with a space inside that can only be filled with Jesus. When we don't have Jesus in our hearts, we go through life trying to find something – anything– to fill this great emptiness. We try to use drugs, food, work, unhealthy relationships, all kinds of harmful things to fill this void, and none of them work. In fact, they enslave us and end up causing more pain, while the hole in our heart just gets bigger.

The good news is that Jesus can deliver us from all of this pain and addiction to harmful things. The definition of deliverance is "to be set free, rescued or released."

When we choose to accept Jesus as our Lord and Savior, He is then able to come in and rescue us. He will set us free from all of the harmful things we unsuccessfully tried to use in our past to take His place.

Now the Lord is the Spirit, and where the Spirit of the Lord is, there is freedom.
2 Corinthians 3:17 (NIV)

Jesus will supernaturally release a spirit of freedom to us, but we have to choose to *walk it out*. This means there are choices we have to make in ourselves, on a daily basis, in order to line our lives up with what is good and healthy. As we do this, He will give us all the strength we need to follow through with these choices, causing change in us.

Prayer

Dear Father God, I thank You for sending Your only Son, Jesus, to pay the price for all my sin and to bring me freedom. Please help me each day to walk out my deliverance from every area of sin in my life, so I can become the person You created me to be. In Jesus' Name I pray, Amen.

Reflection

What choices can I start making in my life to walk out my deliverance from addiction and other areas of sin?

Scripture Reading

Isaiah 61 & John 8:32, 36

Hope

For I know the plans I have for you, declares the Lord,
plans to prosper you and not to harm you,
plans to give you a hope and a future.
Jeremiah 29:11 (NIV)

Isn't that good to hear? God loves us and has a plan for our future! What an awesome declaration of His love for us. All we have to do is give our lives to Him and He is ready to set His good plan for our future in motion.

He forgives all my sins
and heals all my diseases;
He redeems my life from the pit
and crowns me with love and compassion.
He satisifes my desires with good things
so that my youth is renewed like the eagle's.
Psalm 103:3-5 (NIV)

No matter how bad our life is or how ugly our past was, God is able to take it and use it all for the good. In everything He helps us to overcome, we will be able to go back and help others who are struggling in the same areas. Just like I have been set free from addiction and I'm now able to share with others how God helped me so they too can experience the same freedom.

All of His promises to us are real. When we make the decision to live for God and follow in His ways, many blessings will follow us.

Philippians 1:6 promises:

We can be confident that God,
who began a good work in us,
will carry it on to completion. (NIV)

Prayer

Father, I thank You for the bright future You have planned for me. Please begin giving me a vision of this future so that I may be filled with hope in You. In Jesus' Name I pray, Amen.

Reflection

What good plans do I believe God may have for my future?

Scripture Reading

Psalm 23 & 103

Word Power

Your tongue has the power of life and death.
Those who love to talk will eat the fruit of their words.
Proverbs 18:21 (NIrV)

One of the most important decisions we can ever make is to only speak positive and uplifting words over our lives and the lives of others.

The words of our mouth actually chart the course of our lives. Make it a point to release words of faith over your life and future. Having faith means having complete trust and confidence in God. So when we speak "words of faith," we are declaring positive words over ourselves or situations that may seem negative, because we believe in God to change it! Even if a situation really looks bad, go ahead and speak life into the present circumstances, in faith that your words will come to pass.

For example, if we go around saying things like, "My life will never change!" then it probably never will. But, if we speak uplifting words like, "I know that with God's help, I can make every change needed to make my life better!" those words open the door for good things to come into your life.

He who guards his mouth and his tongue
keeps himself from calamity.
Proverbs 21:23 (NIV)

Instead of a negative framework, speak words that will frame your life positively. If you will make a conscious effort to only release positive words that bring life, you will see what a great difference it will make!

Prayer

Heavenly Father, I ask that You please set a guard over my mouth so that I will only release words that bring life to my family and me. Whether good or bad, help me to always remember the power of my words. In Jesus' Name I pray, Amen.

Reflection

Instead of negativity, what words of faith can I now begin
to release over myself and loved ones?

Scripture Reading

Proverbs 13 & Philippians 4:6-8

Shame Free

Instead of their shame my people will receive a double portion,
and instead of disgrace they will rejoice in their inheritance,
and so they will inherit a double portion in their land
and everlasting joy will be theirs.
Isaiah 61:7 (NIV)

This verse is saying that God will take away the shame of our past and replace it with a double portion of all that is good, such as health, prosperity, love, joy, peace, and total restoration in all things! As His children, we have an inheritance of spiritual, physical, and financial blessings. Our land is the redeemed life that God has given us to live. He's saying we will be fruitful and instead of shame, everlasting joy will be ours!

I think the most painful result of drug addiction is the broken relationships with our family members, especially our children. So often, we allow the shame and guilt attached to this pain to keep us in bondage (slavery to drugs).

God has already forgiven us. He forgave us as soon as we asked Him. Now we also need to forgive ourselves and let go of all the shame and guilt. Jesus was sent by God to become a sacrifice and pay a price we could not pay, so all of our sins could be forgiven. In doing this, He also took on *all* of our guilt and shame.

When we are able to lay down our guilt and shame at the feet of Jesus where it belongs, God will be able to begin restoration in our relationships with our family and help us learn how to start loving ourselves.

Blessed are they whose transgressions (sins)
are forgiven, whose sins are covered.
Blessed is the man whose sin the Lord will
never count against him.
Romans 4:7-8 (NIV)

If God, Himself, has forgiven us and forgotten our sin, then who are we to withhold forgiveness from ourselves?

Prayer

Father, please help me to let go of all the shame and guilt that is attached to my past. Thank You for bringing healing and restoration in my relationships with my children and other family members. Thank You for helping me to start loving and forgiving myself. In Jesus' Name I pray, Amen.

Reflection

What are places that I need to forgive myself?

Scripture Reading

John 5 & Jeremiah 31:34

A New Mind

Do not conform any longer to the pattern of this world,
but be transformed by the renewing of your mind.
Then you will be able to test and approve what God's will is –
His good, pleasing and perfect will.
Romans 12:2 (NIV)

One of the main keys to *walk it out* is the renewing of our mind. Reading God's word and learning to apply it in our daily lives begins to create a new mind in us.

So often, as new Christians, we start out with self-destructive thinking patterns and negative mind-sets. But as we spend time every day with God in prayer, hearing His heart for us, and reading His Word, a beautiful transformation begins to take place. We find that we are living and acting more like Christ each day!

Listen, accept what I say,
and the years of your life will be many.
I guide you in the way of wisdom
and lead you along straight paths.
When you walk,
your steps will not be hampered;
when you run, you will not stumble.
Hold on to instruction, do not let it go;

guard it well, for it is your life.
Proverbs 4:10-13

When we focus on God and follow His instruction, before we know it, our lives begin to line up with what His will is for us. As we surrender to God He works in us, enabling us to live good lives that are pure in every way—this is His desire for us, so we can receive all of His blessings upon our lives. When we begin to follow God's commandments and live by His values, we will truly begin walking in real freedom.

Prayer

Dear God, please help me to stay focused on You and Your Word, so that my mind can be renewed and my life transformed by YOU. I want to live a life before You, that is pure in every way, so I can receive all of Your blessings upon my life. In Jesus' Name I pray, Amen.

Reflection

What negative mind-sets and thinking patterns in my life need to be transformed?

Scripture Reading

Proverbs 4 & Romans 8:6-8

You Can Beat It!

Submit yourselves then to God.
Resist the devil,
and he will flee from you.
Come near to God
and He will come near to you
James 4:7 (NIV)

To "resist the devil", means to refuse to sin when he brings temptation to you. It is not a matter of *if* we run into temptation, but *when* we run into temptation. When we do, we need to be prepared.

This is another reason it is important to read the Word and spend time with God daily. It is what gives us the strength to resist the enemy (Satan) when he comes at us, trying to lure us back into sin.

Jesus knows what it is like to be tempted and He will help you.

Because He Himself suffered,
He is able to help
those who are being tempted.
Hebrews 2:18 (NIV)

Matthew, chapter 4, tells the story of how Jesus was led into the desert to be tempted by the devil. Every time the devil tried to tempt Him, Jesus used the written scriptures to overcome it. He used the Word of God!

We wake up every morning and pray for God to continue to give us the strength to stay clean and sober. Throughout the day, we keep our mind on all the things that are good and pure and when the enemy comes, tempting us to go back to our old habits, we pray for Jesus to help us. We remind the devil, "I've been delivered from that and there's no going back! My life belongs to Jesus now!" He has no choice but to flee.

Prayer

Lord Jesus, I choose to submit myself to You and resist the devil. I know if I continue to do this in the face of temptation, the enemy will have no power over me! In Jesus' Name I pray, Amen.

Reflection

What can I do to resist the enemy in the face of temptation?

Scripture Reading

Matthew 4 & 1 Corinthians 10:12-13

My Walk

_____

_____

_____

_____

_____

_____

_____

_____

_____

_____

_____

_____

_____

_____

My Walk

_____

_____

_____

_____

_____

_____

_____

_____

_____

_____

_____

_____

_____

Daily Decrees

1. I will receive, believe, and act on the Word of God!

2. I take my every thought captive into the obedience of Jesus Christ.

3. I have the mind of Christ! I come into agreement with God's thoughts about me!

4. My God will supply all my needs!

5. God is my solid foundation and I will build my life upon Him.

6. God has given me a sound mind. I will make good choices that bring me Life.

7. God has set me free from addiction!

8. I have hope for my future because God has promised me a future beyond what I ever could have imagined!

9. I will spend time daily, reading the Word of God.

10. I go to God in faith that He will answer my prayers, according to His will for my life. I know He desires all the very best for my life.

Wonderful Truth

If you continue in My Word,
then you are my disciples indeed;
and ye shall know the truth and
the truth shall make you free.
John 8:31-32

The Word of God is the truth. In order for the truth of the Word to bring freedom to our lives, we must first receive it. Then we must attach our faith to it and truly believe it. This means we have to put our unquestioning confidence and complete trust into the Word of God that we receive. Then, we can put our faith into action by applying it in our everyday lives. We must live by what we learn to be the truth.

When we build our lives on truth, we are building our lives on an eternal foundation. circumstances will come and go and things all around you may change, but God's word never changes. This world is temporary, but God is forever! He does not make mistakes or change what He says. We can believe Him beyond what anything else looks like or what anyone else may say. Our God does not lie.

Just reading the Bible is not enough. As you begin to understand the truth that is in the Word, you will want to make changes in every part of your life!

The Holy Spirit will guide you through this transformation. He makes us aware of thoughts we may have, or things we say or do that are not like Him. He does not do this to bring shame upon us, but to bring holy change to our lives.

As we begin to transform into who God planned for us to be, we will begin to experience true freedom.

Prayer

Dear God, please help me to receive, believe, and act upon the truth that is in Your Word, so that I may begin to experience true freedom. In Jesus' Name I pray, Amen.

Reflection

In what ways could I begin to put the Word of God I have received, into action in my daily life?

Scripture Reading

Proverbs 6 & Joshua 1

Battlefield

We are at war and our mind is the battlefield.
The weapons we use are not of this world.
They are mighty through God to the pulling down of strongholds.
We demolish arguments and every pretension that sets itself up
against the knowledge of God, and we take captive every thought
to make it obedient to Christ.
2 Corinthians 10:4-5 (NIV)

A negative stronghold is something that tries to hold us in captivity (keep us in sin), such as negative mind-sets and wrong belief systems.

Throughout the day, we may have thoughts that do not line up (or agree) with the Word of God and His commandments. We must immediately take these thoughts captive to the obedience of Christ. We take thoughts captive by coming out of agreement with them because they are not of God. We make a conscious decision to reject the unwanted thought because we know it will bring negative consequences if we act on, or even entertain it. Our weapon in doing this is the supernatural strength we receive from Jesus to withstand the temptation. He will meet us in our decision to reject unclean thoughts and help us to carry it through, as we choose to believe truth. As we learn and consistently practice this key of what to do with unclean thoughts, they will occur less and less often.

You will keep in perfect peace
him whose mind is steadfast,
because he trusts in You.
Isaiah 26:3 (NIV)

Prayer

Father God, please help me to immediately take every thought, that is not of You, captive into the obedience of Christ. Thank You that You are giving me the mind of Christ and that all my thoughts can be brought into agreement with how YOU think! In Jesus Name I pray, Amen.

Reflection

What thoughts have I had lately, that I can take captive into the obedience of Christ?

Scripture Reading

1 Peter 5 & 2 Peter 2:9

Finances

*But my God shall supply all your need
according to His riches in glory by Christ Jesus.
Philippians 4:19*

Often in our addiction, we end up losing almost everything we own. Most of us feel blessed to come out of it alive. Starting over is never easy, but to me it is an adventure!

Matthew 6:33 tells us that when we learn to put God first in our lives, then everything we need will be added to us. This does not mean we won't have to work, but it does mean that God will bless us with a good job. He will give us favor with our bosses. Our money will go far. Our every need will be met according to God's promises. We will even be able to be a blessing to others.

When we are *responsible* with our jobs and everything else we are given, it continues to lay a path for goodness to come into our lives. It is very important for us to be diligent in our jobs and in all that we do.

God knows how much we put into everything, and He loves to honor faithfulness!

We have access into God's presence and His promises at all times. When we need something, all we have to do is call it in! If we need a job, a car, a house, whatever it may be, we can take it to God in prayer, and faith and He will meet our every need. Some things will come more quickly than others, but God *is* faithful and He *will* take care of you.

Prayer

Father God, I have faith in You. You see me and lovingly care for me. You know my every need and You will supply all of my needs, according to Your riches in glory, by Christ Jesus. Please help me to be responsible in my job and in everything You trust me with. In Jesus' Name I pray, Amen.

Reflection

Do I trust that God will meet all of my needs?
Am I responsible with everything that God has blessed me with?
How could I be more responsible?

Scripture Reading

Deuteronomy 28,
Matthew 6:31-33 & Psalm 34:10

Come Out of That Pit!

He lifted me out of the slimy pit, out of the mud and mire;
He set my feet on a rock and gave me a firm place to stand.
Psalm 40:2 (NIV)

If you are still struggling with addiction, in any way, ask God for help and He will give you the strength you need to come up out of that pit!

We must surrender our lives to Him 100% in order for His power to be fully effective in bringing us freedom. This means we have to give Him *everything*. We can't hold back little pieces of our lives that we still want to control.

We also have to be willing to let go of *all* sin in our lives, not just the drugs. If we have any sin left in our lives, it leaves the door wide open for the devil to come and tempt us with drugs again. For example, if we quit doing drugs, yet continue to have sex outside of marriage, this sin separates us from God and gives the devil a legal right to come in and mess with us. This doesn't mean that God doesn't love us when we sin, it just takes us out of alignment with Him and all He wants to give us. Sin ties His hands in bringing us our full freedom and restoration. And He really wants us to be free!

When we submit ourselves to Him, God will lead us in the right direction and give us a strong foundation to build our lives upon.

He will be the firm foundation
for their entire lives.
He will give them all of the wisdom,
knowledge
and saving power they will ever need.
Respect for the Lord is the key
to that treasure.
Isaiah 33:6 (NIrV)

If you are having thoughts about using drugs, don't keep it to yourself! Take the thought captive into obedience to Christ (2 Corinthians 10:5) and ask God to give you the strength to withstand the temptation. It is also wise to call on some fellow Christians, who know about your situation, and get them to pray with you. There is no shame in reaching out for help!

Remember: Put your trust in the Lord. He will not fail you.

Prayer

Jesus, I thank You for delivering me from addiction. Thank You for setting my feet upon a rock and giving me a firm place to stand. Please help me surrender my life to You 100%, so Your power will be fully effective in bringing me freedom. In Jesus' Name I pray, Amen.

Reflection

Is there anything left in my life that I need to fully surrender to God?

Scripture Reading

Psalm 107 & Romans 6:22

This is Your Mind on Jesus

For God has not given us a spirit of fear,
but of power and of love and of a sound mind.
2 Timothy 1:7

You may have heard the expression, "Insanity is doing the same thing over and over again expecting a different result."

This is the type of insanity most of us have experienced, time and again, in our addiction, as we told ourselves the same lies over and over. "This time I won't go too far" or "This time I won't lose everything" and each time we hit rock bottom again.

The good news is we no longer have to walk in this kind of deception! As Christians, we have supernaturally been given the spirit of a sound mind and we no longer have to believe the lies of the enemy, but we have to *choose* to walk in this freedom.

To *walk it out* in the power of a sound mind, means we will no longer act on "insane thoughts" the enemy tries to give us. For example, when he tries to tell you, "One more time won't hurt you" or "You can use drugs this once and get by with it," you will know the truth! You will know and understand that you can never use drugs again and that if you were to use drugs even once,

it would cause too much damage to everything you have worked so hard with God to achieve. It is *never* worth it!

Then you will know the truth
and the truth will set you free.
John 8:32 (NIV)

As we learn to walk in the freedom of God's love and our deliverance from drugs, we begin to understand the truth: We have been set free and we no longer have to carry the fear of relapse. We will continue to move forward and not backward!

Prayer

Heavenly Father, please help me to remember that as one of Your children, I have been given the supernatural power to walk in the freedom of a sound mind. This means that I no longer have to act on "insane" thoughts or carry the fear of relapse. Thank You, for helping me to continue to move forward. Because of You, I never have to go backward again. In Jesus' Name I pray, Amen.

Reflection

What are "insane" thoughts I have been having, that I can take captive into submission to Jesus?

Scripture Reading

Psalm 91 & Proverbs 3:25-26

Our Lifeline

Like babies that were just born,
you should long for the pure milk of God's Word.
It will help you grow up as believers.
1 Peter 2:2 (NIrV)

It is true. Just as newborn babies need milk to survive; Christians get life from reading and meditating on God's Word. Every day, we need to spend as much time as possible in Scripture. This is God speaking to us! The Bible teaches us who God is and who we are. It reveals God's heart for us, and how He loves us. His word gives us the instruction and guidance we need to live in joy, peace, and release from sin that would like to hold us captive!

The more we learn God's heart, read His instructions to us in His Word, and apply it in our lives, the stronger we become as Christians. We will begin to walk in new areas of freedom each day.

In the Bible, the Lord gives us wisdom and understanding of how to live our lives in a way that will be a blessing to others and ourselves.

My son, attend to My words;
incline thine ear unto My sayings.
Let them not depart from thine eyes;
keep them in the midsdt of thine heart;
for they are life unto those that find them
and health to all their flesh.
Proverbs 4:20-22

I know life gets busy with all kinds of responsibilities, but it's important to set a special time aside each day to spend reading God's words. His Word is our lifeline. It will help keep us connected to God and everything He desires to do in our lives.

Prayer

Amazing God! Thank You for Your Word, that I can read and learn Your heart and mind, teaching me to be all You've created me to be. No matter how busy I get, help me to always remember how important it is to spend time with You, each day, so I can grow stronger in every area of my life. In Jesus' Name I pray, Amen.

Reflection

Am I setting time aside each day for the Word of God?
How could I make more time for this?

Scripture Reading

John 8 & Psalm 119:105

Prayer Muscle

*Therefore I tell you, whatever you ask for in prayer,
believe that you have received it, and it will be yours.*
Mark 11:24 (NIV)

When we go to God in prayer, we can always have confidence and faith in Him that He will answer our prayers, according to His will.

Faith believes and trusts in God, knowing that He is real even though we cannot see Him.

*Now faith is being sure of what we hope for
and certain of what we do not see.*
Hebrews 11:1 (NIV)

We see in Romans that one way we can develop our faith is by reading the Word of God.

*So then faith cometh by hearing and hearing
by the Word of God.*
Romans 10:17

As you pray, allow your imagination to see the picture of your answer. If we can see it, we can have it!

As long as we believe in Him, and what we are praying for lines up with the Word and the will of God, He *will* answer our prayers. Of course, when we pray for things that are not of God or within His will for us,

He will not answer these prayers. For example, if we were to pray for a certain mate that God knows would not be healthy for us, or for a certain job that He knows would not be best for us, then He would not answer these prayers because He loves us so much! He always has the *best* for us.

It is always God's will for us to be in good health and to prosper. These are things we can pray for in confidence that it is within His will. As time goes on, and we become more knowledgeable about God and His Word, we will have greater understanding of how and what to pray.

Everything is possible for him who believes.
Mark 9:23 (NIV)

Prayer

My Father, each day please teach me how to pray, and to have faith in You. Thank You, that You care for me and that You only bring me what is best for my life. You will answer my prayers, accordingly. Please continue to increase my faith in You. In Jesus' Name I pray, Amen.

Reflection

What are some things I can begin to pray for in greater faith,
knowing that God will answer according to His will and love for me?

Scripture Reading

Mark 11 & Hebrews 11:6

My Walk

_____

_____

_____

_____

_____

_____

_____

_____

_____

_____

_____

_____

_____

My Walk

_____

_____

_____

_____

_____

_____

_____

_____

_____

_____

_____

_____

_____

Daily Decrees

1. I can do all things through Christ, who gives me strength.

2. I am more than a conqueror through Christ.

3. I will center my life on Christ and care for the needs of others.

4. I forgive everyone who has ever hurt me, including myself.

5. I will love others without conditions.

6. I have the supernatural peace of Jesus in my mind at all times.

7. I am a new creation in Christ! The old is gone and the new has come!

8. I reject a spirit of condemnation, guilt, or shame. I receive forgiveness.

9. The light of Jesus lives inside of me and I will let it shine out to others.

10. I will receive guidance and leadership from my fellow Christians, who will help keep me accountable for my life and actions.

Strength in Christ

I can do all things through Christ who strengthens me.
Philippians 4:13

At times, life can feel overwhelming. During these hard times, it may seem like an uphill battle. But, when things look impossible, we must remember that all things are possible with Jesus.

The Bible says that God will never give us more than we can handle (1 Corinthians 10:13). We are also told, in Romans 8:37, that we are "more than conquerors" through Christ!

It is vital to continually go to God in prayer at all times. Especially when we feel like we are under pressure, we must draw our strength from the Lord. We weren't created to be "under" anything, but to always be "overcomers" through Christ. We are created to be victorious!

When in prayer, ask God to fill you with His supernatural strength. His strength will enable you to face and overcome every problem or difficult situation that comes your way. You can also pray for Him to take away the worry and stress that might try to overwhelm you in the midst of hard circumstances. Pray that He fill you with His peace. He's faithful!

Along the way, we will find a lot of things that are too difficult to face alone, but with Jesus on our side, we will always make it through.

Prayer

Lord, You are bigger than anything I face! When I am feeling overwhelmed with life's problems, I will always draw my strength and comfort from You. Help me to remember that with You on my side, I can do all things! In Jesus' Name I pray, Amen.

Reflection

What are problems or difficult situations in my life that I have been trying to face alone? Why don't you take some time and invite Jesus into those areas.

Scripture Reading

Psalm 31 and Isaiah 43:2

Day 16

You First

Love is not rude, it is not self seeking, it is not easily angered
and it keeps no record of wrongs.
1 Corinthians 13:5 (NIV)

A big part of our transformation, as Christians, is learning how to love others in a healthy and pure way. Healthy love does not place conditions on love. Pure love does not have a "what's in it for me?" mentality. It is not God's heart for us to do something in the name of love, if we are really just doing it for what we expect in return.

When we were living in addiction, we made a lot of selfish choices that hurt both ourselves and those around us. We have to forgive ourselves for our past mistakes, but we must also change our behavior and start making better choices. Part of that, is to cast aside our selfish behaviors and learn to think of the needs of others.

It will take time to build trust with our loved ones. As they see that we have truly changed and are doing our best to to be unselfish, our relationships will become stronger.

It's not that we are to neglect ourselves in any way, rather we are changing from being self-centered to Christ-centered. When I am Christ-centered, I consider the needs of others and am willing to say, "you first."

God loves each one of us unconditionally and He asks us to love others the way He loves us. When we experience His amazing love, we want it to flow out of us to others! God makes it possible for us to really love.

Prayer

Loving, Heavenly Father, please help me cast off my old selfish behaviors and begin considering the needs of others more. Thank You for Your forgiveness and Your unconditional love! Help me to forgive others like You have forgiven me and teach me how to love others the way You love me! In Jesus' Name I pray, Amen.

Reflection
Do I consider the needs of others as well as my own?
Do I love others unconditionally?

Scripture Reading
1 Corinthians 13 & Matthew 6:14-15

Peace

Peace, I leave with you, my peace I give unto you;
not as the world giveth, give I unto you.
Let not your heart be troubled, neither let it be afraid.
John 14:27

When we are coming out of addiction, our minds can be constantly plagued with bad thoughts and memories from our past. I know I had a huge battle with racing thoughts in the beginning, especially at night when I would lay down to sleep.

I learned to overcome these racing thoughts by meditating on scripture and by calling on Jesus to bring me comfort and peace of mind.

When we are harrassed with unsettling thoughts from our past, we can pray for Jesus to fill our minds with His perfect peace, and He will.

Do not be anxious about anything,
but in everything, by prayer and petition,
with thanksgiving, present your requests to
God. And the peace of God, which tran-
scends all understanding, will guard your
hearts and minds in Christ Jesus.
Philippians 4:6-7 (NIV)

The peace of God cannot be completely understood because it is supernatural. But it is very real, and we can actually feel it come over us when we pray.

As you *walk it out*, God will begin to heal your memories. You will remember the bad things less and less and be able to focus more on the good things in your life.

Prayer

Lord, You are the Prince of Peace! Set me free from racing thoughts of my past and help me to receive the peace of Jesus. I thank You for the healing work that You have begun to do on my memories. Help me to remember less and less of the bad things from my past, and begin to focus more on the good things in my life. In Jesus' Name I pray, Amen.

Reflection

When I am plagued with bad thoughts and memories from my past,
how can I access the peace of Jesus?

Scripture Reading

Isaiah 26 & Romans 15:13

Brand New

Anyone who believes in Christ is a new creation.
The old is gone! The new has come!
2 Corinthians 5:17 (NIrV)

When we give our lives to God, we become new creatures in Christ. Romans 6:6 says that we are no longer slaves of sin, because what we used to be, was nailed to the cross with Jesus. We get to start all over with a fresh, clean slate. Isn't that awesome?!

I will give you a new heart
and put a new spirit in you;
I will remove from you,
your heart of stone
and give you a heart of flesh.
Ezekiel 36:26 (NIV)

What this means is that God will take away our stubborn hearts and give us hearts that obey Him. Walking in obedience with Him will lead to a happier, healthier life for us. Praise the Lord! With Him all things are possible!

So when the devil comes around, trying to throw your past up in your face, just remind him, "I'm a new creature in Christ! The person that did those things no longer exists!"

Prayer

Oh, Jesus, I thank You for cleansing me from my past! I know that I am now a new creature in Christ. The old is gone and the new has come! Please remove my stubborn heart and give me a new heart that will obey You. I want to obey You in all things so I can be close to You and have a happier, healthier life. In Your Precious Name I pray, Amen.

Reflection

How does my life show I have become a new creation in Christ?

Scripture Reading

Romans 6 & Deuteronomy 5:33

No Condemnation

Therefore, there is now no condemnation for those who are in Christ Jesus,
because through Christ the law of the spirit of life
has set us free from the law of sin and death.
Romans 8:1 (NIV)

Condemnation is a sense of unworthiness, guilt, or shame. We do not have to feel condemned by our past or our human weaknesses. Jesus has already paid the price for all of our sin on the cross. He was crucified for our sins, so that we might receive forgiveness. All we have to do to receive this forgiveness, is ask God to forgive us and then turn away from that sin.

We need to confess our sins and ask forgiveness so that God can cleanse our conscience. We have to learn to accept God's forgiveness and let go of shame and guilt.

We have no righteousness in and of ourselves, but through the blood of Jesus, we have been made righteous.

One definition of righteousness is "to be morally right, fair, and just." Through the blood of Jesus, we are able to become all of these things! God does not see our past sin or our shortcomings, but our righteousness in Jesus.

Christ didn't have any sin,
but God made Him become sin for us,
so we can be made right with God
because of what Christ has done for us.
2 Corinthians 5:21 (NIrV)

Prayer

Jesus, in You I am righteous! I choose to no longer receive a spirit of condemnation. I choose to accept the sacrifice You made for me. I ask and receive forgiveness of my sins. I understand that through You, I am made morally right. In Your wonderful Name I pray, Amen.

Reflection

In what areas have I been carrying a spirit of condemnation
that I can now release and accept God's forgiveness?

Scripture Reading

Philippians 3 & Romans 3:24-26

Beacons

In the same way, let your light shine in front of others.
Then they will see the good things you do.
And they will praise your Father who is in heaven.
Matthew 5:16 (NIrV)

As Christians, we have the light of Jesus living inside of us, and He asks that we let it shine out to the world in our daily lives.

As you walk out a life free from addiction, you will actually become a "walking testimony" to others. Your testimony is the actual proof and evidence of Jesus others will see in your daily life, as you show them how much you have changed because of Him. People will begin to see the way you have changed and they will praise the Lord for it.

The path of the righteous
is like the first gleam of dawn,
shining ever brighter
till the full light of day.
Proverbs 4:18

I know when I got clean and started living for God, people could tell something was different just by looking at me. They were amazed at the difference God had made in my life and they still are.

We can even use the word of our testimony (our story of deliverance) to lead others to Christ. When they know where we came from, and they see what God is doing for us in our lives, they are going to want what we have and we will be able to tell them just how to get it!

Prayer

Lord, I thank You that Your Holy Light shines out of me wherever I go. Please help me to use this as a testimony to lead others to Christ. Help me to always shine my light! In Jesus' Name I pray, Amen.

Reflection

How can I use my personal testimony to help lead others to Christ?

Scripture Reading

Matthew 5 & Daniel 12:3

Guidance

Follow the lead of one another because of your respect for Christ.
Ephesians 5:21 (NIrV)

Life can be difficult, especially when you are starting over. It is important that we understand that we do not have to do it all on our own. God is always with us and He will also send brothers and sisters in Christ to help teach and guide us along the way.

Two are better than one,
because they have a good return
on their work:
If one falls down, his friend can help him up.
But pity the man who falls
and has no one to help him up!
Ecclesiastes 4:9-10 (NIrV)

Change is a process. In this process it is important to be open to the guidance and teachings of fellow Christians who have more knowledge and experience living for God. They will help us find our way.

Forming relationships with fellow Christians helps us have more accountability for our actions. They will be able to help steer us back in the right direction if we start to fall in some area.

As time goes by and we become more grounded in Christ, we, too, will be able to help lead others on their journey.

As iron sharpens iron,
so one man sharpens another.
Proverbs 27:17 (NIV)

Prayer

God, I will humble myself before You and others. Please help me to always be open to the leadership and teachings of my fellow Christians, so that I may grow more in You each day. In Jesus Name I pray, Amen.

Reflection

What people do I know that could help guide me in my walk with the Lord?

Scripture Reading

Proverbs 12 & Hebrews 10:24-25

My Walk

_____

_____

_____

_____

_____

_____

_____

_____

_____

_____

_____

_____

_____

_____

My Walk

_____

_____

_____

_____

_____

_____

_____

_____

_____

_____

_____

_____

_____

Daily Decrees

1. Spending time with God is my top priority.

2. I will spend time each day reading God's Word.

3. I will praise the Lord at all times.

4. Sin does not have dominion over me!I have authority and power in Christ Jesus over Satan, my enemy!

5. I have faith in God that all of my loved ones will be saved.

6. I will show all the people in my life unconditional love and forgiveness.

7. I will cast all my worries, anxieties, cares and concerns each day upon the Lord
.

8. In all these things, I will trust in Him to take care of me.

9. I will live free from worry!

10. God forgives all my sins and heals all my diseases!

Don't Choke

*But the worries of this life,
the deceitfulness of wealth and desires for other things come
in and choke the Word, making it unfruitful.
Mark 4:19 (NIV)*

We must be very careful not to allow our desire for the things of the world to come in and take God's place in our heart.

If we give more of ourselves and our time to other things, such as television, the internet, and other relationships, neglecting our spiritual life (time spent with God in prayer and the Word), then the Word of God we have in our heart will no longer produce fruit (effect positive change) in our lives. We are then in danger of falling back into our old patterns of sin.

That's not to say we cannot spend any time at all in doing other things, but we must keep it in the proper balance. Spending that intimate time with God is not only a joy, but also our top priority.

We must be cautious not to let life's worries, or the desire for things of the world to take over and keep us from spending time with God. It is so important to spend time face-to-face with Him. As you have that close time together and open your heart to Him, you will become more and more like Him! Consistently seek Him, with all your heart and soul, in order to keep growing in your relationship with Him. It is our relationship with Jesus that gives us life and makes us strong.

Prayer

Wonderful Father, please forgive me for all the times I have spent more of my time in things of the world, neglecting my time with You. Help me to never again get caught up in the worries and desires for other things that will take me away from our time together. Help me to keep my life centered on You. In Jesus' Name I pray, Amen.

Reflection

Have I been neglecting my face-to-face time with God?
Are there other things that have taken too much of my focus?

Scripture Reading

Mark 4 & Psalm 119:9-16

You Can Change the Atmosphere

I will bless the Lord at all times:
His praise shall continually be in my mouth.
Psalm 34:1

Praise changes the atmosphere. When we begin to praise God, the environment (our immediate surroundings) literally changes for the better!

It is an important key in our spiritual growth to continually praise the Lord throughout each day. We praise Him because He is more than worthy of our praise; but praising Him also releases more of His blessings into our lives.

Praise is actually a seed for harvest! Harvest is a time for gathering in crops. So when we praise God, we are planting spiritual seeds that will bring in spiritual crops! These crops will be God's strong presence in our lives along with the blessings that His presence always brings.

When you praise the Lord, just begin by expressing your thanks to Him for who He is, all the good He has done for you in your life, and all that He is going to do in your future!

For example, you could start out by saying, "God, you are so good! Your love for me is amazing! You are so worthy to be praised! I thank You for blessing me! Thank you for saving me and changing my life forever! I love You Lord!" Continue in this way, pouring out your praises to Him. You might like to sing along with a good praise and worship CD, or make up a song of your own! He loves *all* your praise, no matter how it sounds or what it looks like.

When you need breakthrough in any situation, begin thanking and praising Him for answering your prayer, even before you see an actual result. Your praise opens the door for Him to intervene in your circumstances and bless you. Praise will open up the heavens for Him to pour out His blessings all over you!

Prayer

Awesome God, I will praise You at all times! Your praise will be continually in my mouth. You are more than worthy to be praised! Thank You for all of my many blessings. In Jesus' Name I pray, Amen.

Reflection

What are some things I can begin praising God for each day?

Scripture Reading

Psalm 147 & Hebrews 13:15

Day 24
Can't Touch This!

Behold, I give unto you power to tread upon serpents and scorpions,
and over all the power of the enemy:
and nothing shall by any means harm you.
Luke 10:19

The "power to tread upon serpents and scorpions" means that we have the power to stand against Satan, our enemy, and all of his attacks. Praise the Lord! The devil actually has no power over us unless we give it to him. The only way we give him power is by having unrepented sin in our lives. Unrepented sin is active sin that we have not confessed or asked forgiveness for. This type of sin in our lives leaves an open door for the devil.

We have authority over Satan because Jesus lives inside of us. Sin does not have dominion (the power to rule) over us! Grab hold of the authority you have been given through Christ Jesus and stand prepared for any attack of the enemy.

Be self-controlled and alert.
Your enemy, the devil, prowls around like
a roaring lion looking for someone
to devour. Resist him, standing firm in the
faith, because you know that your brothers
throughout the world are undergoing the
same kind of sufferings.
1 Peter 5:8-9 (NIrV)

When we are faithful to spend time with God each day in prayer and in His Word, focusing on living obediently before Him, we will be prepared for anything that comes our way.

Prayer

Father God, please forgive me for any time I have left open doors for the enemy, by having unrepented sin in my life. Please give me the will to pray and stay in the Word each day, so I may be prepared for any attack of the devil in my life. You are greater than anything in this world! I thank You for the power and authority You have given me, in Christ Jesus, to stand strong against any attack. In Jesus' Name I pray, Amen.

Reflection

Is there sin in my life that I need to repent of, so I can close all doors to the enemy?

Scripture Reading

James 4:7 & Colossians 1:13

Family Promise

They replied, "Believe in the Lord Jesus.
Then you and your family will be saved."
Acts 16:31 (NIrV)

If you have unsaved family members, the Bible says to pray for them, believing in God for their salvation and they will be saved.

It may not always come as quickly as we would like, but it will happen. God's timing is not always our timing, but His timing is always perfect. God wants every single one of us to be saved.

The Lord is not slow in keeping His promise,
as some understand slowness.
He is patient with you,
not wanting anyone to perish,
but everyone to come to repentance.
2 Peter 3:9 (NIV)

When you are praying for your loved ones to be saved, you are actually praying God's perfect will!

Believe and trust in God's faithfulness to His promise. He will send them witnesses to share the truth of the gospel of Jesus Christ in a way that they will understand it. You can share Jesus with them as well, but be careful not to do it in a way that is pushy or overbearing. Share Jesus with them in love, then back off and let them make their own decision. The greatest witness will be when they see how much God has transformed your life.

So, go ahead and begin praising and thanking God for the salvation of all of your loved ones! Praise Him every day for their salvation in advance because eventually, you will see it happen!

Prayer

Oh God, I thank You and praise You, in advance, for all of my loved ones being saved. Thank You that You love them even more than I do! Thank You for putting laborers in their path to witness to them about Jesus. Please give me Your perfect wisdom on how and when I should witness to them, as well. In Jesus' Name I pray, Amen.

Reflection
How can I live a good example for my unsaved loved ones
that would make them want to know Jesus?

Scripture Reading

Acts 3 & Luke 19:10

Day 26

Healing Love

Above all, love each other deeply,
because love covers over a multitude of sins.
1 Peter 4:8 (NIV)

As you begin to rebuild your life, it will take time to repair broken relationships. In addition to prayer, the main thing you can do each day is show your family and friends how much you love them. Actions speak louder than words.

Don't be discouraged in continuing to do everything you can to love and show how much you care about them. Keep expressing how important having a good relationship with them is to you. It is important to stay humble in this. Be careful not to act like they suddenly owe you something because you have decided to change. We have to prove it with consistency! We need patience in this process. Just because *you* know where you are, doesn't mean everyone else is on your time-line.

God has forgiven us of so much! Let's also be forgiving when others hurt or don't understand us. They may still have unresolved anger with us from the past that God will heal over time. Continue to live a Jesus life, regardless of what others may say or do. A negative response does not give us the right to respond back in the same way. Remember, you are now able to love freely!

We can't erase the past, but we can overcome it by changing the way we relate with the ones we love. It will take a while to heal the wounds we have created in others, and ourselves, but with God it can be done.

Nobody should seek His own good,
but the good of others.
1 Corinthians 10:24 (NIV)

As we begin to cast off our old self-serving behaviors and focus more on serving others, they will begin to see how much we love them, and healing will begin to take place.

Prayer

I thank You, Father—You are the redeemer and healer of relationships! Lead me in this process. Please, remove selfishness from me. Teach me how to serve and love others, in a way that is healthy and pure, so wounds from the past can be healed and relationships can be restored. In Jesus' Name I pray, Amen.

Reflection

What are some things I can begin doing to rebuild trust
and restore relationships with my loved ones?

Scripture Reading

Isaiah 40 & Romans 8:25

Day 27

Me, Worry?

Who of you by worrying can add a single hour to his life?
Matthew 6:27 (NIV)

Worry is actually a sin because when we worry, we are not trusting in God. We can hand over all our worries, anxieties and fears to the Lord and trust Him to take care of all the things that concern us.

> *Cast all your anxiety on Him*
> *because He cares for you.*
> *1 Peter 5:7* (NIV)

Sometimes, we have to do this more than once in the same situation. When you have given a problem to God and it feels like the worry is trying to creep back in, immediately stop and pray. Give the problem right back to Him again as many times as you need to.

> *Be anxious for nothing,*
> *but in everything by prayer and supplication,*
> *with thanksgiving,*
> *let your requests be made known to God;*
> *and the peace of God,*
> *which surpasses all understanding,*
> *will guard your hearts and minds through*
> *Christ Jesus."*
> *Philippians 4:6* (NKJV)

God doesn't want you to go around suffering with worry. He has made a way for you to be free of anxiety. His desire for you is to enjoy the perfect peace that comes from trusting in Him. You can overcome anxious thoughts by choosing to face each one and giving it to God in prayer. You can also decree specific words of God from the Bible over each concern. You can decree the Scriptures on this page, as well as many other verses in the Bible on trusting God. As you decree these truths over each situation, your trust in God will begin to grow and the worry and anxiety will start to slip away.

Prayer

Lord of Comfort, please forgive me for the sin of worry. Remind me to turn all of my cares over to You in prayer. Thank You, that I can trust You to take care of me in every situation, so I may enjoy Your perfect peace. In Jesus' Name I pray, Amen.

Reflection
In what areas have I been worrying, instead of trusting God to take care of me?

Scripture Reading
Psalm 37 & Isaiah 26:3

Our Healing God

Praise the Lord, O my soul, and forget not all His benefits –
Who forgives all your sins and heals all your diseases.
Psalm 103:2-3 (NIV)

Praise the Lord! We don't have to put up with sickness and disease in our bodies! The Bible does not say He will heal some of our diseases, it says He will heal *ALL* our diseases.

If you or one of your loved ones is having problems with sickness or disease, bring it before the Lord and ask Him for healing. When you pray for healing, pray in faith, believing that God hears you and He will answer your prayer.

It is also good to have other believers come into agreement with us as we pray for healing.

If anyone is sick,
he should call the elders of the church to
pray over him and anoint him
with oil in the name of the Lord.
James 5:14 (NIV)

It is not God's desire for any of His children to suffer with sickness or disease. We can have faith in Him that He will heal us. If you or your loved ones aren't healed immediately, don't be discouraged. Just keep on praying and believing, until you see it happen. Sometimes we have to contend (battle) for it.

Prayer

You are a healing God! I thank You that when I or my loved ones are being attacked by sickness, we can come to You with prayers of faith, and You will heal us. Please help me to grow stronger each day in my faith. In Jesus' Name I pray, Amen.

Reflection

Who do I know, that I can begin to pray for their physical healing?

Scripture Reading

Mark 16 & Jeremiah 30:17

My Walk

_____

_____

_____

_____

_____

_____

_____

_____

_____

_____

_____

_____

_____

_____

My Walk

_____

_____

_____

_____

_____

_____

_____

_____

_____

_____

_____

_____

_____

_____

_____

Daily Decrees

1. I will be faithful to the Lord in my tithes and offerings.

2. Because I am faithful in my giving, I will live in the "Blessing Zone!"

3. I will remain sexually pure in thought, word, and deed.

4. Jesus has set me free from every type of bondage to sin.

5. I will honor the Lord in all my ways and celebrate my freedom!

6. I am an overcomer by the blood of the Lamb and the word of my testimony!

7. I will keep my thoughts only on things that are good and uplifting.

8. Jesus in me is greater than any temptation!

9. The Lord gives me all the strength I need to stand strong in the face of temptation.

10. I will be responsible and work hard in my home, my job, and my relationships with God and my loved ones.

The Joy of Giving

Bring the entire tenth to the storerooms in my temple.
Then there will be plenty of food. Put me to the test says the Lord.
Then you will see that I will open up the windows of heaven.
I will pour out so many blessings that
you will not have enough room to contain it.
Malachi 3:10 (NIrV)

We have given all of ourselves to the Lord. This means we also trust Him with our finances. All that we have is His, but God only asks for 10 percent of what we earn to be given into the place we are spiritually fed. This is called our tithe. It says to God that we trust Him with our money too. It is a joy to give, when we know God has given us so much--we can never out-give Him! He blesses us for honoring Him with our obedience and trust where our finances are concerned, and pours out more than what we could ever give!

We may also include an extra offering to the Lord. We can give this extra offering at our church. Or, you may like to give to another ministry; one that blesses you and others by sharing the gospel in other lands, feeding the poor, caring for orphans and others who are suffering around the world. We can ask God to lead us in where to give.

When you honor the Lord with your tithes and offerings, you will begin to see the difference it will make in your finances. God will begin to pour financial and spiritual blessings out upon your life and you will have more than enough to meet your needs. God will also keep the enemy from attacking your finances.

Don't be discouraged if the blessings don't come immediately. Sometimes they do, but if not, continue to have faith in God and His promises. Remain faithful in your giving; the blessings will come eventually.

Give and it will be given to you.
A good measure, pressed down,
shaken together and running over,
will be poured into your lap.
For with the measure you use,
it will be measured back to you.
Luke 6:38 (NIV)

Prayer

Wonderful Lord, You've given me everything! I love Your generosity and want to be giving like You! I will honor You with my tithe of 10 percent and also with special offerings wherever You lead me to give. I thank You in advance for blessing my finances! In Jesus' Name I pray, Amen.

Reflection

Spend time meditating on the great generosity of God.
What does it mean that He has given me everything?

Scripture Reading

Malachi 3 & 2 Corinthians 9:6-8

Day 30

Sex Talk

Flee from sexual immorality.
All other sins a man commits are outside of his body,
but he who sins sexually sins against his own body.
1 Corinthians 6:18 (NIV)

As a new creation, it is very important for us to abstain from all sexual sin. God meant for sex to be only within the covenant (bonds) of marriage (1 Corinthians 7:2).

Do you not know that your body is the temple of the Holy Spirit, who is in you, whom you have received from God?
You are not your own;
you were bought at a price.
Therefore honor God with your body.
1 Corinthians 6:19 (NIV)

When we commit sexual sins against our own body, we are also sinning against the Holy Spirit who lives inside of us!

This includes pornography. It is harmful to look at any form of pornography whether it is on the Internet, or in books, television, etc. It brings us back into bondage, when God wants us to be free! God's Word warns us to keep ourselves pure. Remember, we have given *all* of ourselves to the Lord. God's instruction teaches us how to *walk out* our freedom and stay safe from sin's traps, keeping us pure in thought, word, and deed.

It is the will of God that you should be sanctified; that each of you should learn to control his own body in a way that is holy and honorable.
1 Thessalonians 4:3-4 (NIV)

You can pray for God to send you the perfect mate to be united with in marriage, and He will, when He sees that the time is right. If you are already married, it is *imperative* that you stay faithful to your partner and God will bless you in your marriage.

God is not trying to deny us something good. These sexual laws are put into place to protect us. He's not keeping us *from* something; He is keeping us *for* something blessed. When we join ourselves sexually to people we are not married to, it damages us emotionally, spiritually, and sometimes physically. It may not be easy at first, but we can pray and ask God to help us stay sexually pure. He will give us the strength we need.

Prayer

Lord, I know that my body is not my own, it is also the temple of the Holy Spirit. I submit my body to Your purposes. Please help me to avoid temptation and abstain from all sexual sin and immorality. In Jesus' Name I pray, Amen.

Reflection
Do I have sexual sin in my life that I need to repent of?

Scripture Reading
1 Corinthians 6 & 1 Peter 2:11

Day 31
Celebrate!

Christ has set us free. He wants us to enjoy freedom.
So stand firm. Don't let the chains of slavery hold you again.
Galatians 5:1 (NIrV)

Jesus came to save us so that we can live free!

He brought them out of darkness and the
deepest gloom
and broke away their chains.
Psalm 107:14 (NIV)

He has set us free from addiction and every type of bondage. Now, we are learning to *walk out* our deliverance. This means following our decision to make Him Lord of our lives with the appropriate changes to our lifestyle. We now make a conscious effort to cut out *all* sin.

When you were slaves to sin,
what benefit did you reap at that time
from the things you are now ashamed of?
Those things result in death!
But now that you have been set free from sin
and have become slaves to God,
the benefit you reap is holiness
and the result is eternal life.
Romans 6:20-22

If we want to truly live in freedom, we must fully submit our lives to the authority of Jesus, following Him in all our ways. We can no longer allow our flesh or human weaknesses to rule us. We are free when we submit our body and our minds to the Spirit of God within us.

If we allow even a little sin to invade our lives, it leaves the door wide open for the devil to come back in and re-enslave us to a life of addiction and every other type of bondage.

This does not mean you will ever be perfect. Only Jesus is perfect. If you make a mistake, repent and move on. You are making choices that bring you life and that means choosing never to live in sin.

So in everything you do, honor the Lord and celebrate your freedom!

Prayer

Dearest Jesus, thank You for the price You have already paid for my freedom. I never want to be enslaved to sin again. I will honor You in all my ways and celebrate my freedom! In Your Precious Name I pray, Amen.

Reflection

Are there ways I need to change my lifestyle in order to walk in true freedom from sin?

Scripture Reading

Romans 8 & 2 Corinthians 3:17

Testimony Power

*They overcame by the blood of the lamb
and the word of their testimony.
Revelation 12:11 (NIV)*

We are all overcomers by the blood of Jesus and our testimony. The Bible calls on us to share our testimony with others. This is very powerful!

*Give thanks to the Lord,
call on His name;
make known to the nations
what He has done.
1 Chronicles 16:8 (NIV)*

This means that not only are we to spread the gospel and the good news of Jesus, but we are also to share our personal testimony as a witness to others of what Jesus can do in a person's life. When we share our testimony, it opens up the door for others to experience the same miracles we have received in our lives.

For example, we can share with others about our past, the mistakes we made and the bad consequences that resulted in our lives. Then, we can share how we came to know the Lord, how much He has blessed and helped us, changing our lives for the better. When others hear about the great things God has done for us, it will fill them with hope that He can do the same for them!

Deliverance from addiction is an absolute miracle! Go out and share what the Lord has done! Not only does it give hope to others, it will make you stronger too!

Prayer

Father, I thank You that I am an overcomer by the blood of Jesus and the word of my testimony. Please fill me with boldness to go out and share with the world the miracle of my deliverance! In Jesus' Name I pray, Amen.

Reflection

Who do I know that could benefit from hearing my personal testimony?

Scripture Reading

Luke 4 & 1 John 5:4-5

Captive Thoughts

*Finally, brothers, whatever is true, whatever is noble,
whatever is right, whatever is pure, whatever is lovely,
whatever is admirable, if anything is excellent or praiseworthy;
think about such things.*
Philippians 4:8 (NIV)

If we go around all day, thinking about things that are negative, we are going to feel pretty bad. Negative thoughts will only keep us down. God wants us to keep our focus on the things that are good so our emotions can be lifted up.

This doesn't mean we don't have to face our problems. But, we are to keep our focus on the solution rather than worrying and meditating on the problem.

Every day we need to bind our minds to the mind of Christ and ask ourselves the question, "Is this the kind of thought Jesus would have?" If not, God intructs us on what to do with those negative thoughts in 2 Corinthians 10:5: "...We take captive every thought to make it obedient to Christ."

This means we intentionally refuse to accept negative thoughts when they knock on our mind's door. This takes practice, but if we make a conscious effort to do it every time, it will begin to come naturally.

It is our responsibility to keep our thoughts aligned with the Word of God. If we change the way we think, we will change the way we live! When we learn to keep our thoughts going in a positive direction it will just make for a better day all around.

Prayer

Father, please help me keep my focus on all the things which are good and uplifting. Help me always focus on the positive rather than the negative. In Jesus' Name I pray, Amen.

Reflection

How can I change my way of thinking, to make it more positive?

Scripture Reading

John 14 & Psalm 23:6

Day 34

Escape Route

*No temptation has seized you except what is common to man.
And God is faithful; He will not let you be tempted beyond
what you can bear. But when you are tempted,
He will also provide a way out so that you can stand up under it.*
1 Corinthians 10:13 (NIV)

When we run into temptation, we can call upon the Lord and He will show us the way out. He will pour His mercy and grace out upon us, supernaturally giving us the strength to walk away from temptation without sinning.

God may do this in different ways at different times. When you are tempted and you go to Him in prayer, He may give you the sudden strength you need to turn the other way without giving in to the temptation. Another time, He may bring to your mind someone you could call to help support you in prayer, or to even come pick you up, wherever you are.

There are also times that the Lord will give you warnings that you feel in your spirit, letting you know that you are headed for trouble. When you feel a warning you can pray it out and avoid the situation altogether!

The Bible tells us that every man is tempted, but if we will submit ourselves to God and resist the devil, he will flee from us (James 1:14; James 4:7). So, when we are tempted, we can ask God for the strength to withstand it and He will give it to us. There is always a way out.

*The Lord knoweth how to deliver
the godly out of temptations...*
2 Peter 2:9a

Prayer

God, You are the greatest! Thank You that no temptation is greater than You in me! I will always call upon Your name when I need extra strength to withstand enticement. Thank You for always having a way out of temptation and showing it to me! In Jesus' Name I pray, Amen.

Reflection

In the future, what can I do to avoid sin in the face of temptation?

Scripture Reading

James 1 & 1 John 4:4

I Want to Eat

People who refuse to work
want things and get nothing;
But the longings of people who work hard
are completely satisfied.
Proverbs 13:4 (NIrV)

God truly wants to bless your life. There are some things we need to do so those blessings can flow freely. God did not intend for us to only sit around and do nothing. We are created for so much more! We even begin to feel badly about ourselves when we neglect our responsibilities and this opens a door to temptation.

We must work in order to provide for our families and ourselves; whether that work is in our homes, caring for the house and children, or in the work force outside.

Anyone who doesn't want to work sleeps
his life away and a person who refuses to
work goes hungry.
Proverbs 19:15 (NIrV)

Rebuilding our lives is going to take a lot of work. We have to work hard at our jobs, as well as rebuild relationships with God and our loved ones. He will give us all the strength we need to meet every task.

Commit to the Lord everything you do
and your plans will succeed.
Proverbs 16:3 (NIrV)

Now, of course this does not mean that we can never have a day off. We also need to take time to rest and relax. We can pray and ask God to help us find a healthy balance in this.

As we become more responsible and productive citizens, we will actually begin to feel much better about ourselves and we will have a greater sense of accomplishment.

Prayer

Father God, please help me to be faithful and diligent in all that is before me. I know You will give me the strength I need to rebuild my life in every way. In Jesus' Name I pray, Amen.

Reflection

Have I been diligent in my work at home or on the job?
Have I been faithful in rebuilding my relationships with God and my loved ones?

Scripture Reading

Proverbs 15 & Colossians 3:23-24

My Walk

_____

_____

_____

_____

_____

_____

_____

_____

_____

_____

_____

_____

_____

_____

My Walk

Daily Decrees

1. I am never alone. I will not be afraid. God is always with me.

2. Change is a process and I know, through Jesus, I can make all of the changes necessary to transform my life.

3. I am confident that Jesus will carry on the good work He has begun in me unto completion.

4. I am highly favored with God and man.

5. I am the head and not the tail. I am above and not beneath; therefore, I will always come out on top of every situation.

6. I will not act out or speak in anger, but I will go to God in prayer, seeking His wisdom when I become angry.

7. I will show honor and respect to all authority figures in my life.

8. Though I enjoy doing good works in God's name, I know that I am not saved by these good works, but by the blood of Jesus!

9. God's ways are not my ways and His timing is not my timing. I choose to have complete faith in His ways and His timing.

10. I know God is always working to bring the best into my life. I will have complete trust in Him to take care of me in every situation.

God, My Friend

So do not be afraid. I am with you.
Do not be terrified, I am your God.
I will make you strong and help you.
My powerful right hand will take care of you.
I always do what is right.

Isaiah 41:10 (NIV)

When we make the decision to change our lives, many times we end up having to leave behind our old friends and sometimes, even our family members because they are not good influences on us.

At first, you might feel like you are all alone in the world-- but this is not true! God is right there with you, walking with you every step of the way! He is everything to you--God is your friend!

When I said, "My foot is slipping,"
your love, O Lord, supported me.
When anxiety was great within me,
your consolation brought joy to my soul.
Psalm 94:18-19 (NIV)

When you feel lonely, you can go to the Lord, and He will fill the void. When you seek Him in prayer, He will always bring comfort in your time of need.

I will not leave you comfortless:
I will come to you.
John 14:18

As time goes on, you will begin to meet new, healthy friends, who also love God. They will be a positive influence on your life. I encourage you to actively seek out these friends in your church or at other Christian gatherings. No matter what happens, God will always be your friend and, unlike human beings, He will never fail you!

Prayer

Oh God, what a joy it is that You call me "friend!" Thank You for being my friend. Continue to teach me how to be a good friend to You. I know that I can always come to You, if I am feeling lonely and You will fill the emptiness inside, and bring me comfort. You are everything I need. In Jesus' Name I pray, Amen.

Reflection
From now on, what can I do when I am feeling lonely and need comfort?

Scripture Reading
Isaiah 54 & Deuteronomy 31:6

Transformers

I am sure that the One who began a good work in you
will carry it on until it is completed.
That will be on the day Christ Jesus returns.
Philippians 1:6 (NIrV)

The "One" this verse is referring to is Jesus. When we give our lives to Jesus, He begins to immediately transform us from the inside out to become more and more like Him. This is a process that will continue in us for the rest of our lives.

Sometimes it may seem like change is not coming fast enough. But, if we will continue to surrender our lives to Him, He will be completely faithful in helping us to make the necessary changes.

As we are in relationship with Him, Jesus will reveal to us things we need to add to or subtract from our lives. There is real reward to being immediately obedient, surrendering everything He reveals to us.

I'm sure you have already made many transitions since you have given your life to the Lord. Continue surrendering everything to Him for the rest of your life. Changes continue! It may seem like a big task, but with Jesus, you have all the strength needed to do everything He asks of you. As you submit yourself in obedience to the Lord, step-by-step your life will be transformed.

Prayer

Dear Jesus, I have complete faith in You! I believe the good work You have begun in me will be carried out for the rest of my life. I know You will reveal to me all needed changes, one step at a time. Thank You for giving me Your strength to carry them out. In Your Holy Name I pray, Amen.

Reflection

What are areas that Jesus has already transformed in my life?
What are other changes He has been revealing to me that I can work on with Him?

Scripture Reading

Philippians 1 & 1 John 2:6

Favor

The Lord will make you the head and not the tail.
If you pay attention to the commands of the Lord your God that I give you this day
and carefully follow them,
you will always be at the top, never at the bottom.
Deuteronomy 28:13 (NIV)

What an awesome and powerful verse that is! It is one of God's amazing promises to us when we follow all His ways.

"The Lord will make you the head and not the tail," means that He will cause you to come out on top in everything He directs you to do in your life. You will have more of His blessings than the rest of the world who is not following after Him. When we are careful to follow the Lord in all our ways, we will receive His absolute favor upon our lives.

He will bless us in our jobs, He will multiply our finances and He will restore and bless our relationships. We will be blessed in all we put our hands to do!

God loves us with unconditional, everlasting love. He wants nothing more than to pour all of these blessings out upon our lives, but we have to hold up our end of the deal! It's not that we have to earn anything with God. These things are all already ours because of Jesus. But when we are walking in obedience, He knows He can trust us with all He wants to give us. God is SO good that He does not want us destroyed by having more than we can bear...even of His goodness.

It is because He loves us so much that we are able to respond in love. One way we express our love is by following His commandments and honoring Him in every area of our life—work, finances, relationships, time, etc.

If we will learn to be faithful in all these things we will begin to see how highly favored we will become with God and man.

Prayer

Dear God, You are so generous! Thank You that I am the head and not the tail. I am above and not beneath! Thank You for the amazing favor You have bestowed upon my life. I will honor You in all my ways. In Jesus' Name I pray, Amen.

Reflection

In what ways has God already shown me favor and blessings in my life?

Scripture Reading

Psalm 1 & Psalm 34:10

Anger

When you are angry do not sin.
Do not let the sun go down while you are still angry.
Don't give the devil a chance.
Ephesians 4:26-27 (NlrV)

In this life, there will be times that we become angry. Anger, in itself, is not a sin. At times, anger is a natural response when people do things to hurt our loved ones or us. The key is not to let our anger cause us to sin with our words, or by acting out in revenge. Anger becomes sin when we do not deal with it, allowing it to become bitterness we hold in our hearts.

When someone does something that causes you anger, learn to take it to the Lord in prayer before you respond. That will help you not to speak words that you will later regret. If you will take the time to stop and pray about the situation, instead of just "flying off the handle," it will give you a chance to calm down and hear God's voice of wisdom on how He would have you handle the situation.

Sometimes, anger has nothing to do with the present situation, but is a result of something unresolved from our past. Always examine this as a possibility, to make sure your anger is not misdirected.

It is very important to never go to bed with unresolved feelings of anger. When we do, it opens up a door for the enemy to come in and cause more havoc in our lives. We do not want to hold on to bitterness and resentment.

Get rid of all hard feelings, anger and rage.
Stop fighting and lying.
Put away every form of hatred.
Be kind and tender to one another.
Forgive each other, just as God forgave you
because of what Christ has done.
Ephesians 4:31-32 (NlrV)

Prayer

Father, please help me to be slow to anger. When I do become angry, please help me not to sin. I know when I come to You, You will give me wisdom on how to handle each situation. In Jesus' Name I pray, Amen.

Reflection

Do I have unresolved anger that I can ask God to help me deal with?

Scripture Reading

Proverbs 16 & Ecclesiastes 7:9

Authority

Obey your leaders and submit to their authority. They keep watch over you
as men who must give an account.
Obey them so that their work will be a joy, not a burden,
for that would be of no advantage to you.
Hebrews 13:8 (NIV)

God has placed people of authority in our lives to guide, guard, and protect us. He asks that we honor and submit to people in these positions. Honoring includes acting respectfully, even when we disagree with them.

The only time we should not submit to an authority figure is if they are asking us to do something that is clearly not of God. In situations like this, always seek counsel from other Christians.

People of authority could be leaders in our church, probation or parole officers, mentors, parents, and even our bosses at work. Of course our bosses or parole officers would not have authority in our spiritual lives, but they are still to be honored.

1 Samuel 15:22 tells us that rebellion is as the sin of witchcraft. When we rebel against figures of authority in our lives, it will only bring us harm.

Many of us have suffered some type of abuse from someone who abused his or her authority. This can make it difficult to trust those positions again, but God will help you to trust. Pray and ask Him to heal any of these past issues. Jesus can be trusted and will help you to trust others again.

Prayer

My Father, please forgive me for any rebellion I've had against the authority You have placed in my life. Please give me a heart that is submissive and not rebellious. Heal me of any wounds caused by abuse from any authority figures in my past and help me learn to trust again. In Jesus' Name I pray, Amen.

Reflection

Do I show honor to all of the authority figures in my life?

Scripture Reading

1 Peter 2 & Colossians 3:20-22

Ahhh, Grace...

*For it is by grace you have been saved, through faith –
and this not from yourselves, it is a gift from God –
not by works, that no one can boast.*
Ephesians 2:8-9 (NIV)

Salvation is not something we can earn by the good deeds we do. Salvation is purely a gift from God. The only way we can obtain this gift is to accept Jesus Christ as our personal Lord and Savior.

*He saved us, not because of righteous things
we had done, but because of His mercy.
He saved us through the washing of rebirth
and renewal by the Holy Spirit, whom He
poured out on us generously through Jesus
Christ our Savior.*
Titus 3:5-6 (NIV)

Being created in the image of God, we are created to do good in all things; this includes good works. When we give our lives to Jesus, we are filled with the desire to do them.

*We are God's workmanship,
created in Christ Jesus to do good works,
which God prepared in advance for us do.*
Ephesians 2:10 (NIV)

Though our salvation is not dependent upon good works, there are still many benefits. They help us to come out of our selfishness, which immediatly causes us to begin feeling better about ourselves. It also becomes a great joy to help and serve others, as we get to see the results of the good works we do reflecting in their lives.

Always remember, that while we do good works in God's name, this is in honor of Him and what He has already done. Our works are a response of love back to God, and not a condition of our salvation.

Prayer

Dear God, I thank You for the gift of salvation that is in Christ Jesus. Please help me to always remember that my salvation is a gift from You, and while I enjoy doing good works in Your name, it is not these, but the blood of Jesus that saves me. In Jesus' Name I pray, Amen.

Reflection

Have I tried to earn my salvation by good works,
rather than accepting it as a gift, that was paid for by the blood of Jesus?

Scripture Reading

Romans 3 & 2 Timothy 1:9

The Perfect Way

For My thoughts are not your thoughts, neither are your ways My ways saith the Lord.
For as the heavens are higher than the earth, so are My ways higher than your ways,
and My thoughts your thoughts.
Isaiah 55:8-9

We may not always understand the way God is working in our lives, but He knows what is best for us and He is always working for our benefit.

God's way is perfect.
The Word of the Lord doesn't have any flaws.
He is like a shield
to all who go to Him for safety.
Psalm 18:30 (NIrV)

When it seems like you have unanswered prayer in a certain area, it may be that God has a different plan, or He could possibly be waiting to answer it in His own perfect timing. Sometimes God has to wait until we are ready. God always knows what is best for us in each situation.

Put your faith and trust in God. He will come through for you, even if it may be in a different way than what you are expecting.

We know that in all things God works
for the good of those who love Him.
Romans 8:28 (NIrV)

This means that as you love God and honor Him, He will take every situation in your life and turn it into something good. Meditate on that truth and let it take root in your heart. It will give you peace in every circumstance.

Prayer

Faithful Father, I know that even though I may not always understand Your ways, You are always working on my behalf. I trust that You will always do what is best for me and my future in You. In Jesus' Name I pray, Amen.

Reflection

Have I put my complete trust in God? Do I know that
He is always going to give me what is best, even though I don't always understand His ways?

Scripture Reading

Isaiah 55 & Romans 4:20-21

My Walk

_____

_____

_____

_____

_____

_____

_____

_____

_____

_____

_____

_____

_____

_____

My Walk

_____

_____

_____

_____

_____

_____

_____

_____

_____

_____

_____

_____

_____

_____

_____

Daily Decrees

1. The Joy of the Lord is my strength!

2. I am an "overcomer" of all problems through Christ Jesus.

3. I take full responsibility for my thoughts. I choose to have only good and positive thoughts!

4. I will honor God in my thoughts and actions.

5. I am one of God's redeemed children!

6. God forgives all my sins and heals all my diseases!

7. I will not try to hide any "secret" sin from God or my loved ones. I know God sees all!

8. I am filled with the Holy Spirit of God!

9. I will submit myself to Christ each day to become more like Him.

10. I will choose to only have Christian friends who will be a positive influence on my life.

Joy, Joy, Joy!

*Weeping may endure for a night,
but joy cometh in the morning.*
Psalm 30:5

God wants to heal us from every wound caused by our past, and He will, if we let Him. God saves us, heals us, and transforms us, but that does not mean all of the consequences of our sin will disappear overnight. Be careful during this process not to become angry with God just because things aren't moving along as quickly as you think they should.

As you begin to fill yourself up with more of Him, you will also be filled with His joy.

The joy of the Lord is our strength.
Nehemiah 8:10 (NIV)

There is a difference between joy and happiness. Happiness is based on outer circumstances and is temporary. Joy is not based on circumstance; it is a condition of the heart and in Jesus, it is everlasting.

With the Joy of the Lord in your heart, you have the strength to stand against all the power of the enemy and be an overcomer of poverty, sin, sickness and disease, and all the pain of your past. Even in the most difficult of circumstances, you can still feel the Joy of the Lord in your heart, when you learn to stay close to Him.

If you don't feel the manifest presence of God's joy in your life, just ask Him to fill you and open up your heart to receive. The Joy of the Lord truly is our strength!

*…Ask and you will receive,
and your joy will be complete.*
John 16:24 (NIV)

Prayer

Dear Lord, I thank You for the joy you have put in my heart that brings me strength in any circumstance. I know that in You, my joy is eternal. In Jesus' Name I pray, Amen.

Reflection

Have I been confusing the joy of the Lord with happiness,
which depends on circumstances?

Scripture Reading

Isaiah 51 & Isaiah 61:3

What Do You Think?

You should obey.
You shouldn't give in to evil longings.
They controlled your life when you didn't know any better.
The One who chose you is Holy. So you should be holy in all you do.
1 Peter 1:14-15 (NIV)

As God's kids, we want to honor Him in everything we say and in everything we do, including our thought life.

If we sit around thinking about doing sinful things, then it won't be long before our actions follow the same pattern. As we learned previously, we must immediately take all sinful thoughts captive into obedience to Christ.

Jesus bore our sins in His body on the Cross,
so that we might die to sin
and live for righteousness;
by His wounds you have been healed.
1 Peter 2:24 (NIV)

In our past, we were controlled by sin because we did not have Jesus. Now that we have made the decision to follow Him, we have to also follow with change. The Holy Spirit will guide us in this process.

Watch and pray
so that you will not fall into temptation.
The spirit is willing, but the body is weak.
Matthew 26:11 (NIV)

It is important to stay alert against falling back into any type of sinful thinking so that our actions will remain pure.

Prayer

Dear God, You are Lord over my life and my thoughts. I want to live before You in a way that is holy and pure. Thank You for walking with me each day, helping me to change so I can be all You created me to be. Help me to keep my thoughts in line with Your will for my life. In Jesus' Name I pray, Amen.

Reflection

Have I been honoring God in my thoughts as well as my actions?

Scripture Reading

Romans 12 & Romans 8:6-8

Redeemed

I will praise the Lord.
I won't forget anything He does for me.
He forgives all my sins. He heals all my sicknesses.
He saves my life from going down into the grave.
His faithful and tender love makes me feel like a king.
Psalm 103:2-4 (NIrV)

God loves us so much! As we learn to walk with Him, we will begin to share in the many benefits of being one of His redeemed children.

Redeemed means: to buy back, to set free by paying a ransom, to be delivered from sin and its penalties, to restore. That's it! We have been redeemed! The blood of Jesus has paid the ransom for us! We have been bought back and now we are being restored.

God forgives all our sins and He remembers them no more. He heals us from all sickness and disease, and He has redeemed our life from the pit! He has untangled us from the chains of addiction and planted our feet on solid ground!

His love for us is truly amazing! He surrounds us at all times with His love and compassion. He loves you so much that He sent His only Son, Jesus, to die on the cross to pay for your sin.

It is good to take some time to meditate on God's great love. Get this truth planted deep down inside, so you can walk in the confidence of how much He loves you.

Prayer

My Loving Father, I know You love me even more than I can comprehend. Please help me get the reality of Your amazing love planted deep within my heart. Thank You for redeeming my life from the pit and planting my feet on solid ground. In Jesus' Name I pray, Amen.

Reflection

What are some of the ways God has shown me His amazing love?
Take some time to soak in how loved you are by your Heavenly Father.

Scripture Reading

Ephesians 3 & Psalm 107:1-3

Turn On the Light

*For nothing is secret that will not be revealed,
nor anything hidden that will not be known and come to light.*
Luke 8:17 (NKJV)

There is nothing we can do that God doesn't know about. We cannot hide our sin from Him. He knows everything. If we try to do things in secret and hide our sin from our loved ones, it will only cause more pain for them and ourselves in the future, when the truth comes out. The truth always comes out eventually. For our own sake, God will make sure it does.

Someone once said, "We are only as sick as our secrets." As long as we are hiding our sin, we are not free to repent and move on with our lives, in the freedom of God's forgiveness.

*Therefore, confess your sins to each other
and pray for each other so that you may
be healed. The prayer of a righteous man is
powerful and effective.*
James 5:16 (NIV)

In order to be free of hidden sin, you have to reveal the truth and ask forgive- ness. In this way the truth will set you free!

*Have nothing to do with the fruitless deeds
of darkness, but rather expose them.*
Ephesians 5:11 (NIV)

If there is any sin in your life you have been trying to hide, please ask God to forgive you! He will give you the strength to come clean with the people in your life. God will help you through this process and you will begin to experience the freedom of forgiveness and truth.

Prayer

Father, I know that nothing I do in secret is hidden from You. Please forgive me for any time I have tried to hide "secret" sin in my life. I know I do not need to hide from You. Please give me the strength to always reveal the truth so I may be set free. In Jesus' Name I pray, Amen.

Reflection

Is there sin in my life I have been trying to hide, that I can confess now
and receive forgiveness?

Scripture Reading

Psalm 32 & Isaiah 55:7

I Speak Heaven

All of them were filled with Holy Spirit
and began to speak in other tongues
as the Spirit enabled them.
Acts 2:4 (NIV)

After receiving salvation, you will also want to pray for God to come and fill you with His Holy Spirit. Speaking in tongues is evidence of being filled with the Holy Spirit and an important gift to help in spiritual growth. Speaking in tongues on a daily basis will actually help build you up and strengthen you spiritually.

Anyone who speaks in tongues
does not speak to men but to God.
Indeed, no one understands him;
he utters mysteries with his spirit.
1 Corinthians 14:2 (NIV)

When we use the gift of tongues, the Holy Spirit is praying through us exactly what needs to be prayed in any situation. This is especially helpful when we are confused about what, or how to pray.

If you desire to be filled with the Holy Spirit and receive the gift of tongues, just ask the Lord. He will come fill you with His Spirit and give you this precious gift. You may also ask other believers, who already have this gift, to lay hands on you and pray with you to also receive it.

Then Peter and John placed their hands on
them and they received the Holy Spirit.
Acts 8:17 (NIV)

If you already have the gift of tongues, use it as much as possible. If not, then seek it with all your heart. It will truly strengthen your walk with the Lord.

Prayer

Dear God, I thank You so much for sending the Holy Spirit to live inside of me, giving me guidance and strength. I also thank You for the precious gift of tongues. In Jesus' Name I pray, Amen.

Reflection

Have I been filled with the Holy Spirit?
If not, would you like to pray that He fill You now, and to receive the gift of tongues?

Scripture Reading

Acts 19 & Ephesians 5:18

Fruit

But the fruit the Holy Spirit produces is love, joy, and peace.
It is being patient, kind, and good.
It is being faithful and gentle and having control of oneself.
There is no law against things of that kind.
Galatians 5:22-23 (NIrV)

What God desires most for our lives, is for us to be like Christ. When Christ lived on earth, His life showed all the fruit of the spirit: Love, joy, peace, patience, kindness, goodness, faithfulness, gentleness and self-control. The more we become like Him, the more we will show the same fruit in our lives.

We become more like Christ by staying in close relationship with Him.

I am the vine, you are the branches.
If anyone remains joined to Me, and I to him,
he will bear a lot of fruit.
You can't do anything without Me.
John 15:5 (NIrV)

You remain in close relationship with Christ by praying throughout the day, talking with Him and recognizing that He is al-ways with you, reading the Word faithfully and applying it in your life, and obeying the Lord's commandments.

You did not choose me. Instead, I chose you.
I appointed you to go and bear fruit. It is fruit that will last. Then the Father will give you anything you ask for in My Name.
John 15:16 (NIrV)

Wow! What an honor it is to be chosen by Him to live a good life that bears much fruit, living in His blessing all of our days.

Prayer

Beautiful Jesus, I want to always stay in close relationship with You. Help me become more and more like You, so that I will produce good fruit that will last. In Your Name I pray, Amen.

Reflection

What is some good fruit that has been produced in my life,
since I have come to know Jesus?

Scripture Reading

Galatians 5 & John 15:9-10

Friend or Foe?

Godly people are careful about the friends they choose.
But the way of sinners leads them down the wrong path.
Proverbs 12:26 (NIrV)

As new Christians, we need to be very careful and use godly wisdom in whom we choose as our friends. It's very important to surround ourselves with people who will have a positive impact on our lives.

Anyone who walks with wise people
grows wise, but a companion
of foolish people suffers harm.
Proverbs 13:20 (NIrV)

If we hang around people who love the Lord and show it in their daily actions, we too will do good; but if we are around people who have loose morals, who are not living for God, we can be led down the wrong path right along with them.

This means not to hang out with people who are drinking, doing drugs, living in sexual sin, stealing, and any other such behavior that is not righteous. We should also stay away from people who just have an over-all rebellious or negative attitude. Attitudes can be contagious!

Once you become stronger and more mature in the Lord, you may be able to be a good influence on them and lead them to the Lord, but you have to be sure you are on very solid ground in your own life first. If you try to go back into those types of situations too soon, it could cause you to fall. Pray, and the Lord will show you when the time is right.

You can also pray for God to guide you in choosing quality people, with good character, as your friends. The Holy Spirit will guide you in making good choices.

Prayer

Father, please give me the wisdom I need to choose good, Christian people to be my friends; people that will be a positive influence on my life. In Jesus' Name, Amen.

Reflection

Do I have friends in my life now, that are a negative influence on me?

Scripture Reading

1 John 1 & Colossians 3:16

My Walk

_____

_____

_____

_____

_____

_____

_____

_____

_____

_____

_____

_____

_____

My Walk

_____

_____

_____

_____

_____

_____

_____

_____

_____

_____

_____

_____

_____

_____

Daily Decrees

1. My words are very powerful and I will be very careful how I use them.

2. I will not engage in gossip or speaking negatively about others or myself.

3. I will put on the "Full Armor of God" each day.

4. I will pray and be watchful at all times.

5. Because I love my children, I will discipline them with godly correction.

6. The past is not my identity!

7. My identity is who I am in Christ!

8. Nothing can separate me from the love of God.

9. I will always show mercy and forgiveness to others.

10. I will be an active part of a good church that helps me learn more about God.

Day 50

Lip-Lock

Those who talk a lot are likely to sin,
but those who control their tongues are wise.
Proverbs 10:19 (NIrV)

Our words are very powerful, so we need to be very careful how we use them. We should never engage in gossiping or talking in a negative way about people and we need to be cautious not to say things to people that belittle them, or make them feel bad about themselves. In the same way, we must never speak badly of ourselves, either.

When we say things like, "I'm so stupid" or "I'm just lazy," we are speaking negative words over our own life. Statements like, "He/she will never change," etc., are negative words over others. We want to steer clear of this kind of speech. We will receive the fruit (effects) of our words, whether good or bad. So, if we choose to speak over others and ourselves in positive ways, then we will see positive results. This is why declaring the Word of God, in our daily decrees, is so important.

Anyone who guards what he says
guards his life.
But anyone who speaks without
thinking will be destroyed.
Proverbs 13:3 (NIrV)

It is a good practice to always think about what we are going to say, before we say it. If in doubt, we should ask ourselves, "What would Jesus think about me saying this?" If we don't think He would like it, let's not say it. Sometimes, it's a good idea to listen more and talk less.

Prayer

Lord, I submit my words to You. Please help me to become more disciplined in the way I speak to, or about others, as well as myself. Please teach me to always think before I speak. In Jesus' Name I pray, Amen.

Reflection

Have I been engaging in gossip or in speaking badly about others or myself?
What kind of Harvest would I like to reap from my words?

Scripture Reading

Matthew 12 & Proverbs 16:23

Day 51

Invincible

Put on all of God's armor.
Then you can stand firm against the devil's evil plans.
Ephesians 6:11 (NIrV)

It is very important for us to put on the full Armor of God each day. It protects us and strengthens our walk with the Lord. What exactly is the "Full Armor of God?" I'm glad you asked!

Let's look at Ephesians 6:14-17

Put the belt of truth around your waist...

To put it simply, be honest with God, yourself, and others.

Put the armor of godliness on your chest...

This means to live our lives in right standing with God, according to His Word, and with a sincere heart.

Wear on your feet what will prepare you to tell the good news of the gospel of peace...

Always be prepared to tell others about the good news of Jesus and the peace, only He can bring.

...Also, pick up the shield of faith. With it, you can put out all of the flaming arrows of the evil one...

Our faith shield guards us against doubting that God is capable of helping us. We hold on to this faith, even when the devil is trying to lie to us and tell us God will not help us.

Put on the helmet of salvation...

This speaks of guarding our minds from our old negative thinking patterns and deceptions from the enemy.

And take the sword of the Holy Spirit, God's Word...

We are to actively apply God's Word to our lives.

At all times, pray... Eph. 6:18

Remember, we learned that prayer is to stay in constant communication with God throughout our day; sometimes, to just acknowledge His presence. He is our constant Friend.

God tells us, that the evil days will come; but if we put on all of God's armor, we will be able to stand up to anything. And, after we have done everything we can, we will still be standing! (Ephesians 6:13)

Prayer

Lord, I thank You for giving me everything I need, to stand against the enemy. Each day I will be sure to put on my full armor that You have given me. In Jesus' Name I pray, Amen.

Reflection

What can I do each day, to make sure I am wearing the "full armor of God?"

Scripture Reading

Ephesians 6 & Isaiah 40:31

Loving Our Children

Those who don't correct their children hate them.
But those who love them are careful to train them.
Proverbs 13:24 (NIrV)

Many times, we as parents allow guilt from our past mistakes to interfere with the way we relate to our children. We cannot withhold correction from them to make up for hurting them in the past. That will only make things worse and create further harm.

We can apologize for the past, where we have fallen short as parents and express our desire for things to be different in the future. Let them know you are going to do your very best to be a reliable Christian parent to them from now on. This includes godly discipline!

A child is going to do foolish things,
but correcting him will drive his foolishness
far away from him.
Proverbs 22:15 (NIrV)

Children have to be taught right from wrong. This can be done in a way that shows love as well as correction. It is very important to be consistent. In the long run, it will help them feel more safe, secure and loved.

When bringing discipline to our children, we must be sure that we are not just reacting to something that has made us angry or afraid. We must respond to the issue and remember to take care of the hearts of our kids.

Just as we do not withhold godly correction from our children, because we love them, we need to understand that God will be the same way with us when we need correction in our lives. Because He loves us, He will bring correction to us, when needed, to steer us back in the right direction.

If you did not grow up with loving correction, you may seek wisdom from others, who can help teach you godly parenting.

Prayer

Thank You, God, for my beautiful children. I ask that You give me wisdom in how to love and discipline them in a godly way. Thank You for full restoration in my relationship with them and for healing their wounds from the past. In Jesus' Name I pray, Amen.

Reflection

Have I withheld godly correction from my children because of guilt from my past? How can I begin to give them good loving correction?

Scripture Reading

Deuteronomy 11 & Proverbs 22:6

New Passport

But because of his great love for us,
God, who is rich in mercy,
made us alive with Christ...
For we are God's workmanship,
created in Christ Jesus to do good works,
which God prepared in advance for us to do.
Ephesians 2:4,10 (NIV)

The past is not our identity! God has redeemed us from our past and now our true identity is who we are in Christ.

Forget the former things;
do not dwell on the past.
Isaiah 43:18 (NIV)

Anyone who is in Christ is a new creation;
the old is gone, and the new has come.
2 Corinthians 5:17 (NIV)

The "new" is who God created each of us to be from the very beginning. This is our identity. He has a wonderful plan for each of us, our futures are secure and we will do amazing works in the name of Jesus!

Satan wants to keep us bound to our past. He desires to make us feel badly about ourselves and to believe we will never be good enough. We must choose to lay the past at the feet of Jesus, and pursue the destiny and inheritance God has for us!

Forget those things which are behind and
reach forward
to those things which are ahead.
Philippians 3:13 (NIV)

This is exactly what we have to do. We have a bright future ahead of us!

Prayer

Heavenly Father, I thank You that my past is not my identity. Please help me to leave my past at the feet of Jesus, where it belongs, so I can move into the future You have planned for me. In Jesus' Name I pray, Amen.

Reflection

What are some facets of my true identity in Christ?

Scripture Reading

2 Corinthians 5 & Titus 3:5

Day 54

Truest Love

*For I am convinced that neither death nor life,
neither angels nor demons, neither present nor the future,
nor any powers, neither height nor depth,
nor anything else in all creation,
will be able to separate us from the love of God
that is in Christ Jesus our Lord.*
Romans 8:38 (NIV)

That's right! No matter what the world throws at you, no matter what comes your way, nothing, absolutely nothing can separate you from the love of God!

*But the Lord is with me
like a mighty warrior...*
Jeremiah 20:11

Once you accept Jesus as your Lord and Savior, He is with you from that moment through eternity. He will be with you always, in good times and bad. He will be with you, even when others fail you. He is your constant, faithful God and Friend. There is nowhere you could possibly go and nothing you could ever do to get away from God, or to make Him stop loving you. His love for you is everlasting!

*Where can I go from Your Spirit?
Where can I flee from Your presence?
If I go up to the heavens, You are there;
if I make my bed in the depths,
You are there.
If I rise on the wings of the dawn,
if I settle on the far side of the sea,
even there Your hand will guide me,
Your right hand will hold me fast.*
Psalm 139:7-10 (NIV)

Prayer

Father God, I thank You for the amazing and everlasting love You have for me. I know You are always with me, no matter what. In Jesus' Name I pray, Amen.

Reflection

Do I truly understand that I can never be separated from God's love?
Take some time and meditate on the depth of His love for you.

Scripture Reading

Psalm 139 & Jeremiah 31:3

Mercy & Forgiveness

Those who have not shown mercy
will not receive mercy when they are judged.
To show mercy is better than to judge.
James 2:13 (NIrV)

When people hurt or fail us in some way, God asks us to show them mercy and forgiveness.

Be merciful just as your Father is merciful.
Luke 6:36 (NIV)

Just as we have been forgiven much by God and our loved ones, we must also forgive others when they hurt or disappoint us. Forgiveness is one of the most freeing things we can do for ourselves. If we hold on to unforgiveness in our heart, it makes it impossible for us to move on with our lives. It keeps us trapped in anger and bitterness. Unforgiveness will harm you more than anything anyone has done to hurt you.

Anyone who claims to be in the light,
but hates his brother is still in the darkness.
Whoever loves his brother
lives in the light and
there is nothing in him to make him stumble.
1 John 2:9-10 (NIV)

Forgiveness is a choice. We may not always feel it, or immediately trust the person who hurt us, but we can trust God to bring healing and to restore these relationships.

Just because we forgive someone does not automatically mean we should trust them again. For example, if someone steals from us, we can forgive them, but that does not mean we immediately leave them unattended around our possessions again. If someone physically abuses us in a relationship, forgiveness does not mean we should automatically take them back into our homes and into our lives. When we seek God, He will give us His wisdom in each situation.

We also need to be very careful not to judge people. Judgment is reserved for God alone. We have all sinned and fallen short in many areas of our lives, so we have no right to stand in judgment of others.

As we learn to walk in mercy and forgiveness toward all people, we will begin to experience a newfound freedom.

Prayer

Merciful God! Thank You for the mercy You have shown to me, and forgiving me of all my sins. Please teach me to always show that same mercy and forgiveness toward others. In Jesus' Name I pray, Amen.

Reflection

Is there anyone who has hurt or disappointed me that I need to forgive?

Scripture Reading

Matthew 6 & 18:21-22 & Mark 11:25

Plug In

Let us not give up meeting together,
as some are in the habit of doing,
but let us encourage one another – and all the more
as you see the day approaching.
Hebrews 10:25 (NIV)

It is very important for us, as new Christians, to get connected with other believers who love the Lord and are working for the advancement of His Kingdom. This is called the body of Christ. One of the best ways for us to do this, is to find a good church that you can attend and feel at home.

It is good for us to spend time each day, building our relationship with God privately, but there is also power in meeting together to learn about God and to praise and worship Him.

Let Christ's Word live in you
like a rich treasure.
Teach and correct each other wisely.
Sing psalms, hymns and spiritual songs.
Sing with thanks in your hearts to God.
Colossians 3:16 (NIrV)

There is truly strength in unity. If you do not already have a home church, find out some information about local churches and ask God to lead you to the one that would be best for you.

In deciding what church is best for you, you will want to make sure the church you choose has an atmosphere of love and acceptance that makes you feel comfortable. God will help lead you to a place that will accelerate your growth in Him.

Remember, what you sow you reap. So, sow into friendship! Don't just wait for someone to come to you and ask you if you'd like to do something with them. Make that first move. Ask the Lord who you might approach to see if they would like to have coffee with you.

Prayer

Dear God, I thank You for the body of Christ. Please lead me to the best place to meet with other believers, have fellowship, and to learn more about You. In Jesus' Name I pray, Amen.

Reflection

Have I found a good church home to attend, where I feel loved and accepted?

Scripture Reading

Acts 2 & Psalm 55:14

My Walk

_____

_____

_____

_____

_____

_____

_____

_____

_____

_____

_____

_____

_____

_____

My Walk

_____

_____

_____

_____

_____

_____

_____

_____

_____

_____

_____

_____

_____

_____

Daily Decrees

1. I can do all things through Christ who gives me strength!

2. With God, all things are possible to one who believes.

3. I will build my inner spirit daily through prayer and God's Word.

4. I will take care of myself properly, but not place too much focus on outer beauty.

5. I will nurture and focus more on my inner beauty.

6. I have the power of the Holy Spirit living inside of me!

7. I get stronger every time I avoid temptation.

8. I will only have godly sorrow that leads to repentance and healthy changes.

9. My life is showered with the blessings of God.

10. I will do all in my power to live in peace with others and avoid strife!

No Limits

I can do all things through Christ who gives me strength.
Philippians 4:13 (NIV)

The key word in that verse from Philippians is *"all."* It does not say that we can do *some* things, but that we can do *all* things through Christ, who gives us strength.

Through our faith in Jesus, we can overcome every obstacle that comes our way.

In this life there will be many problems that we do not have the strength to face alone, but with Jesus, all things are possible. We are more than conquerors through Christ Jesus. Nothing is too hard for Him (Romans 8:37).

When we find that our faith is too small to grasp this truth, it is time for us to spend more time in the Word, hearing the truth of how big our God is! Spend time in prayer, asking the Lord to increase your faith.

So faith comes from hearing the message; and the message that is heard is the Word of Christ. Romans 10:17 (NIrV)

In other words, if you feel like you are facing some huge, immovable mountains in your life, circumstances that you don't think you can overcome; find the scriptures that speak to you about how to conquer the problem. Focus on the Word of God and declare what God says about these problems, instead of staying focused on how impossible it may seem. If we stop focusing on the problem and start believing in the solution (God), good things will begin to happen!

Prayer

Oh God, You're so amazing! I thank You for the power You have given me, through Jesus, to face and overcome every problem that comes my way. Please help me keep my focus on You and Your Word as the solution, rather than staying focused on the problems. In Jesus' Name I pray, Amen.

Reflection

Do I need to change my way of thinking, to focus more on God and His Word
as my solution, instead of dwelling on my problems?
What are some specific problems that I can begin believing in Him to help me resolve?

Scripture Reading

Psalm 121 & Nahum 1:7

Day 58

Spiritual Gym

When a man won't work the roof falls down.
When his hands aren't busy the house leaks.
Ecclesiastes 10:18 (NIrV)

To be strong enough to stay free from drugs, we must build our spirit. We do this by spending that good quiet time with Jesus, reading His Word, hearing His heart and sharing our heart with Him. We need to do this daily; it makes our spirit strong and that is our only source of true strength. Our spirit loves truth! So study the Word of God, memorize it, meditate on it, and apply it!

The blood of Jesus has set us free, but we have some things to do in order to *walk it out!* We can't afford to sit back and think there is nothing else we have to do. We need to keep ourselves and our families covered in prayer and keep ourselves full of God's Word, so when the enemy does come at us with temptation, we are strong enough to face it and overcome it.

Never stop reading this Scroll of the Law. Day and night you must think about what it says.

Make sure that you do everything that is written in it.
Then things will go well with you.
And you will have great success.
Joshua 1:8 (NIrV)

When you discipline yourself to spend time each day in His presence, you will experience how wonderful God is, how He talks with you and just loves you. You will actually start to develop a hunger for that time of being with Him in prayer and reading and hearing His Word, and it will come more naturally.

Prayer

Father, please help me to be faithful in building up my inner spirit. Give me a deep hunger to spend more time with You in prayer, and in reading Your Word. In Jesus' Name I pray, Amen.

Reflection

Have I been faithful in building up my inner spirit, through spending time with the Lord each day?

Scripture Reading

1 Peter 1 & Isaiah 40:8

Inner Beauty

Braiding your hair doesn't make you beautiful.
Wearing gold jewelry or fine clothes doesn't make you beautiful.
Instead, your beauty comes from inside you.
It is the beauty of a gentle quiet spirit.
Beauty like that doesn't fade away.
God places great value on it.
1 Peter 3:3-4 (NIrV)

Much of the time, our society places too much value and importance on outside appearance. In today's world, it is easy to get caught up in that trap, but true beauty really does come from the inside.

This does not mean that we don't care or put time into our outward appearance. Of course we should take care of ourselves and God wants us to feel good about ourselves, but we have to keep it in balance.

So much is missed when we are judged, or we judge others, according to how they look. Learn to look at a person's heart and character, rather than the way they dress or how good looking they are.

It is a good idea to ask Holy Spirit to show us any negative attitudes or character weaknesses we may have, that take away from our inner beauty. He will help reveal them to us and then we can pray for God to help us change in these areas, increasing our inner beauty.

Also, recognize in yourself the areas that already bring strength to your inner beauty. It's important to focus on the positive as well as the negative. We can build upon the good qualities we already have to make them stand out even more. Good looks will come and go, but inner beauty never fades away...in fact, we just becomes more beautiful!

Prayer

Lord, please help me not to put too much emphasis on the outward appearance of others or myself. I want to always remember that true beauty comes from the inside. You are beautiful in me! In Jesus' Name I pray, Amen.

Reflection

In what ways can I work on my attitude and character,
to strengthen and bring out my inner beauty?

Scripture Reading

1 Peter 3 & Philippians 1:6

Training

So I say, live by the Holy Spirit's power.
Then you will not do what your sinful nature wants to do.
Galatians 5:16 (NIrV)

Every human being is born with a sinful nature, but with the power of the Holy Spirit we can overcome it. In and of ourselves we do not have the power to withstand temptation, but with the Holy Spirit, who lives inside of us, we can stand up to anything.

When we are faced with any kind of temptation, we can always pray, in order to tap into the power that we already have resident inside of us.

The Bible also tells us that the flesh is trained by practice (Hebrews 5:14). I have found this to be very true in walking out my own deliverance from addiction. Every time I overcome any form of temptation, it gets easier and easier to avoid it the next time.

For example, when I quit doing drugs, the devil would try to entice me to go back and use again. Every time, I would pray for strength and refuse to give in to that temptation. I grew stronger and stronger each time until finally, the temptation to use was gone altogether.

So in the face of temptation, we can draw upon the power of the Holy Spirit by prayer, reading God's Word, and decreeing it (speaking it out loud). Each time we put this into practice, we are actually training our flesh to live in obedience to God.

Prayer

Father God, I thank You that I can always draw upon the power of the Holy Spirit, who lives inside of me, for strength in times of temptation. I know that every time I overcome any temptation, it makes me stronger and more prepared for the future. In Jesus' Name I pray, Amen.

Reflection

How will I handle temptation the next time it comes?

Scripture Reading

Hebrews 4 & 2 Peter 2:9

Godly Sorrow

*Godly sorrow brings repentance that leads to salvation and leaves no regret,
but worldly sorrow brings death.*
2 Corinthians 7:10 (NIV)

There is a big difference between godly sorrow and worldly sorrow. With godly sorrow, you see where you have gone wrong and ask God to forgive you. Then you turn away from that sin and make the necessary changes (repentance).

Worldly sorrow does not produce change. It only causes shame and guilt, which leads to more oppression from the enemy. Shame and guilt are not from God.

God does not want us to sin and He doesn't want us to live with condemnation over sins that have been forgiven.

*Therefore, there is now no condemnation
for those who are in Christ Jesus,
because through Christ Jesus
the law of the Spirit of life set me free
from the law of sin and death.*
Romans 8:1-2 (NIV)

This means there is no judgment of guilt on us because we no longer walk after the flesh, but after the spirit. We now live by the law of our *new* being, which is who we are in Christ. The law of sin and death is the law of our old being, which no longer exists, because we have been born again in Christ!

When Jesus died for us on the cross, He paid the price for all our sins so that we may have forgiveness. In order to receive this forgiveness, all we have to do is believe in Jesus and the work of the cross, ask for forgiveness, and receive it. We then have to turn away from our sin and begin to live obediently.

Jesus said, "It is finished!" with His last breath in John 19:30, which means it is paid in full! Our sins are totally forgiven.

Prayer

Father, what an incredible gift You have given to me! I thank You for sending Your Son, Jesus, to pay the price for all my sin. Please set me free from all condemnation and produce in me a godly sorrow that will lead to repentance. In Jesus' Name I pray, Amen.

Reflection
Has the sorrow I have felt over my sin led to repentance and change?

Scripture Reading
John 5 & John 8:10-11

Benefit Package

Blessed are all those who have respect for the Lord.
They live as He wants them to live.
Your work will give you what you need.
Blessings and good things will come to you.
Psalm 128:1-2 (NIrV)

There are many benefits we will receive because we are God's children and we honor Him in all our ways. God is a perfect Father, Who takes care of His family in every way.

He will cause us to be successful in our jobs, He will bring restoration to our relationships, He will give us peace that surpasses all understanding (Philippians 4:7), He will heal us of all the wounds caused by our past, and He will give us strength to overcome all obstacles. Whatever we are in need of, we can take it to Him in prayer with faith that we will receive it.

And He will give us anything we ask.
That's because we obey His commands.
We do what pleases Him."
1 John 3:22 (NIrV)

When we are careful to live each day before God, in a way that is holy and pure, continuing to submit our lives to Him, walking in the power of what Jesus has done for us, He will pour more blessings out upon us than we are able to contain!

We must understand that all these blessings will not appear all at once. All of the blessings of Heaven are already ours but we will see some more quickly than others. Again, God is a good father. He knows when the time is right for His kids to receive what He has for them. As we continue to honor our Father God by believing all He says, growing and maturing in Him, we will reap the benefits of being in His household.

Prayer

Heavenly Father, I thank You for the many blessings You have already given me and for the ones yet to come. I know You will continue to help me to walk before You in a way that is pure and blameless in Your sight. In Jesus' Name I pray, Amen.

Reflection

What are some of the blessings God has already given me?

Scripture Reading

Deuteronomy 11 & Exodus 23:25-26

Perfect Peace

So let us do all we can to live in peace.
And let us work hard to build each other up.
Romans 14:19 (NIrV)

As God's kids, it is very important for us to walk in peace with one another, to have gentleness and meekness toward all men, avoiding strife. We should do all in our power to build each other up and not tear each other down!

Ask the Holy Spirit to help you not become easily angered or offended by anyone, but follow after peace instead.

> *Tell them not to speak evil things*
> *against anyone.*
> *Remind them to live in peace.*
> *They must consider the needs of others.*
> *They must be kind and gentle*
> *toward all people.*
> *Titus 3:2 (NIrV)*

God has shown each of us so much forgiveness and patience. He asks that we, in turn, be forgiving and patient with one another.

This does not mean we are to let people run all over us. Healthy boundaries are good! We don't have to let people take advantage of us, or violate our standards, according to our belief system. At the same time, we should seek to walk in God's perfect love with everyone at all times and do whatever it takes to keep things peaceful.

Prayer

God, thank You for Your patience with me. Please help me to also be patient and follow after peace instead of strife. I want to always walk in Your perfect love with all people. In Jesus' Name I pray, Amen.

Reflection

Have I been doing everything I can to avoid strife and keep things peaceful with others?

Scripture Reading

Ephesians 4 & Matthew 5:44

My Walk

_____

_____

_____

_____

_____

_____

_____

_____

_____

_____

_____

_____

_____

_____

_____

My Walk

_____

_____

_____

_____

_____

_____

_____

_____

_____

_____

_____

_____

_____

Daily Decrees

1. I will have patience in my recovery process. Progress will be made one step at a time.

2. I am grateful for God's amazing mercy and forgiveness!

3. I will turn away from all sin and make the necessary changes in my life.

4. God will restore for me all the years the devil stole in my addiction.

5. God will bring full restoration to my life in every area: physically, emotionally, and spiritually.

6. I will wait to date, until I have learned to love others and myself in a way that is healthy and pure.

7. When I begin dating, I will choose to date someone who loves Jesus with all their heart.

8. I have a future and a hope in Jesus!

9. I will not tell lies. I will choose to be honest with everyone at all times.

10. I will set aside a special time each day to spend quiet, alone time with God.

Joy in the Journey

The strength to keep going
must be allowed to finish its work.
Then you will be all you should be.
You will have everything you need.
James 1:4 (NIrV)

Progress in our recovery is made one step at a time. We have to exercise our patience in this because impatience will only make us miserable. Try to enjoy every phase of this process, even though you will experience some discomfort.

Another fruit of impatience is that it sometimes causes us to give up.

You need to persevere
so that when you have done the will of God,
you will receive what He has promised.
Hebrews 10:36 (NIV)

When we continue to press through, we *will* come into God's plans and purposes for our lives. You've already begun! Don't be discouraged by comparing yourself to someone else or wishing you are "farther down the road." God is with you *here*. He loves you and will continue to lead you in this process. Much of the "process" is building your relationship with Jesus. Get all the treasure that is in *this* place and you will be richer as you continue on the journey.

We did not develop all of our wrong mindsets and thinking patterns over night. These are things we have been doing for years. Don't expect to be perfect in everything all at once or you will become overwhelmed. Just continue to walk and build your relationship with the Lord, making the changes that need to be made in order to honor Him and have your life filled with the goodness only He can bring! Study the Word of God and act upon it-- you will become the person He always planned for you to be.

Prayer

Dear God, I thank You that You will complete the good work You have begun in me. Please give me the wisdom and patience I need to make the changes I need to make, one step at a time and one day at a time. In Jesus' Name I pray, Amen.

Reflection

Where can I have more patience with myself in my recovery process?
Have I begun making the changes that will bring goodness into my life?

Scripture Reading

Hebrews 10 & Hebrews 6:12

OOPS!

*Let the wicked forsake his ways
and the evil man his thoughts.
Let him turn to the Lord and He will have mercy on him
and to our God for He will freely pardon.
Isaiah 55:7 (NIV)*

*No one can say, 'I have kept my heart pure.
I'm clean. I haven't sinned.'
Proverbs 20:9 (NIrV)*

Everyone makes mistakes. If we fall down in some way, no matter how big or small, God is still there. We can turn back to Him and repent of our sin. He will forgive us and give us the strength to move on.

If we fall into sin in any area, we must turn away from it quickly! The ground we have won is too precious to give it back to the enemy. There is no "safe" sin. The longer we allow any type of sin to penetrate our lives, the more solid ground we lose.

*...Let us throw off everything that hinders
and the sin that so easily entangles,
and let us run with perseverance the race
marked for us. Hebrews 12:1 (NIV)*

God is right there, ready and willing to forgive, and take us back into His loving arms to restore us. We do not have to be trapped by sin any longer!

*It is for freedom
that Christ has set us free.
Stand firm, then, and do not let yourseves
be burdened again by a yoke of slavery.
Galatians 5:1*

Prayer

Father God, once again, I thank You for Your amazing mercy and forgiveness. Please reveal to me anything in my life that is displeasing to You. Give me the strength and will to lay it down, and turn away from it. I want to obey You in every way. In Jesus' Name I pray, Amen.

Reflection

Is there anything in my life that I need to lay down,
turn away from, and receive God's forgiveness?

Scripture Reading

Ephesians 1 & 2 Chronicles 30:9

Restored

I will repay you for the years the locusts have eaten,
my great army that I sent among you.
You will have plenty to eat, until you are full,
and you will praise the name of the Lord your God,
who has worked wonders for you;
never again will people be shamed.
Joel 2:25-26 (NIV)

God will repay all of the years the enemy robbed from us while we were in our addiction. He will restore us in every way and accelerate our growth in Him, to make up for the years we lost.

He will help build up our lives with Him as our foundation. Then nothing will be able to shake us. He will make sure that we become financially secure and that all our needs are met, physically, emotionally and spiritually.

In Him, we will lack nothing. The shame and guilt of our past can be forgotten and we will come to know the true Joy of the Lord!

I am with you
and I will watch over you wherever you go,
and I will bring you back to this land.

I will not leave you
until I have done what I have promised you.
Genesis 28:15 (NIrV)

That is good news to hear because God always keeps His promises!

Prayer

Faithful God, I know that You will repay all the years I lost to my drug addiction. Thank You for the work of restoration You have begun in me. I know You are faithful to restore all that has been stolen by sin. Thank You for restoring me, physically, emotionally, and spiritually, and for removing all the shame of the past. In Jesus' Name I pray, Amen.

Reflection

What am I believing God to restore for my family and me?

Scripture Reading

Psalm 66 & Joshua 23:14

Watch Those Yokes

Do not be yoked together with unbelievers.
For what do righteousness and wickedness have in common?
Or what fellowship can light have with darkness?

2 Corinthians 6:14 (NIV)

When we first get clean from drugs, it is good that we wait a while before we begin dating. During this time, God can teach us how to love others and ourselves in a way that is healthy and pure.

When we do start to date again, it is imperative that we do not date unbelievers. If we do, it could set us back dramatically. People who have not submitted their lives to Jesus have a totally different set of values and principles. If we choose to date a non-believer, then we will end up compromising all of our own godly values.

When deciding whether to date someone, we should ask them if they know Jesus. Then look for the fruit of God's spirit in their lives: love, joy, peace, patience, discipline, goodness, morals, faithfulness, honesty, and self-control.

Before entering into a relationship, you will want to make sure that *both* of you have been healed of all past wounds and issues. You don't want either of you carrying baggage from your past into the relationship.

If either of you have not been healed, it will end up being a very unhealthy relationship. Both of you should also be willing to make a commitment to yourselves, each other, and God to stay sexually pure in the relationship. When you truly care about someone, you don't want sin to come between either of your relationships with God.

We've asked Jesus to be Lord of our life and we have given Him 100-percent of who we are. He will add to us! Let's not take our dating life back into our own hands. We know our Father has the very best to give us. We can trust Him in this area too. Let's submit our relationships to the Lord.

When we make the good decision to choose a believer to be our mate, God can truly bless our union.

Prayer

Father, please give me wisdom about when it is okay for me to begin dating again. When the time comes, guide me in choosing the right person to date and marry. In Jesus' Name I pray, Amen.

Reflection
Am I allowing God to heal me of all my inner wounds before I begin dating?
Is the relationship I'm in now, a healthy one?

Scripture Reading
2 Corinthians 6 & Hebrews 13:4

Hope Lives

Praise be to God the Father of our Lord, Jesus Christ!
In His great mercy He has given us new birth
into a living hope
through the resurrection of Jesus Christ from the dead.
1 Peter 1:3 (NIV)

Praise the Lord! The hope we have is alive because of the work of the cross! This hope is not dependant on what we can do in and of ourselves, but on what we can have and do because of *Jesus*, who lives within us.

...Christ in you, the hope of glory.
Colossians 1:27

...We who have fled
to take hold of the hope offered to us
may be greatly encouraged.
We have this hope as an anchor for the soul,
firm and secure.
Hebrews 6:18-19

To activate this hope in your own heart, attach your faith to what Jesus has already done for you, so you can receive every promise God has given you. When we attach our faith, we are actively choosing to believe God's Word, using it in every situation where there is a need.

'For I know the plans I have for you,'
declares the Lord,
'plans to prosper you, and not to harm you,
plans to give you a hope and a future.'
Jeremiah 29:11 (NIV)

When we were born again, by accepting Jesus into our hearts and making Him Lord of our lives, we stepped right into that hope for our future. It is absolutely ours for the taking! In fact, it has been freely given!

Prayer

Heavenly Father, I thank You for the precious hope I have been freely given, as one of Your redeemed children. Please help me to attach my faith and activate this hope in my everyday life. In Jesus' Name I pray, Amen.

Reflection

What are some of the hopes I have for my life?
What plans do I think God may have for my future?

Scripture Reading

Proverbs 3 & 2 Corinthians 9:8

Straight Talk

Do not lie to one another,
for you have stripped off the old self with its evil practices.
Colossians 3:9 (NIrV)

We have been called to be set apart from the way the world lives. This means we are to live righteous and honest lives. If we want to build trust with God and our loved ones, we cannot be in the habit of lying, or being deceptive in any way. A lie is a lie, no matter how great or how small.

We cannot rebuild our lives upon a foundation of lies. God loves us and He truly wants to bless our relationships, but we have a responsibility. This includes being completely honest at all times. When we learn to value the truth, we will be made free by it.

Lies also leave an open door for the enemy. So, if there is anything you have been dishonest about, seek forgiveness and make it right by owning up to the truth in each situation. God will give you the strength and the wisdom you need to do this.

He guards the path of those who are honest. He watches over the way of His faithful ones. Proverbs 2:8 (NIrV)

Prayer

Dear God, forgive me for all the lies I have told in the past. Please help me to be honest at all times and to value the truth, so I can walk in the freedom truth brings. In Jesus' Name I pray, Amen.

Reflection

Are there lies I have told that I need to make right?

Scripture Reading

Proverbs 2 & Ephesians 5:21

Shh...Let's Be Quiet

*My people shall dwell in a peaceable habitation,
in safe dwellings, and in quiet resting places.
Isaiah 32:18*

Quiet time, spent alone with God, is very healing to our soul. Oh, that we would all take a special time each day, just to get by ourselves, away from all of the busyness of our everyday lives and have quiet alone time with Him! He loves to spend time with you and looks forward to your quiet times together.

Prayer and Bible study is vital to your spiritual growth, but you also need to spend time in quiet meditation, allowing what you have read in the Word, or heard Him speak to soak into your heart. Take the time to think on Who He is, and all He has done. This is when you will be able to hear from God more clearly. You may want to have a journal with you, so you can write the things God says to you.

Quiet time also helps you to rest your mind and restore your peace and tranquility. God's heart is for all of us to live in a place that is safe and peaceful. Let's not forget to take time out to just rest and enjoy it.

*Be still and know that I am God...
Psalm 46:10 (NIV)*

Prayer

Wonderful God, I thank You for bringing me into a safe place of peace and rest in You. Please teach me how to enjoy times of quiet rest, so that I may hear Your voice more clearly. In Jesus' Name I pray, Amen.

Reflection

Have I been taking a special time each day for quiet, alone time with God?

Scripture Reading

Psalm 91 & Isaiah 26:3

My Walk

_____

_____

_____

_____

_____

_____

_____

_____

_____

_____

_____

_____

_____

My Walk

_____

_____

_____

_____

_____

_____

_____

_____

_____

_____

_____

_____

_____

_____

_____

Daily Decrees

1. I will focus on changes in my own life and be merciful to others.

2. I will help others by living my life as an example of God's goodness!

3. I will make wise choices that will bless my future.

4. I will listen to the warnings of the Holy Spirit when I am headed in the wrong direction.

5. I will put all my trust in God!

6. I will forever give God all my praise and thanks for what He has done in my life!

7. I know there is safety in the Lord.

8. I will pray for those in darkness to come to the light of God.

9. I will be a "Fisher of Men" by leading others to the Lord.

10. God's greatest desire is to have relationship with me. I am very precious to Him.

Ouch! Something's in My Eye

Why do you look at the speck of sawdust in your brother's eye
and pay no attention to the plank in your own eye?
Matthew 7:3 (NIV)

We need to be very careful not to focus on what needs to be changed in the lives of others, but on what needs to be corrected and changed in our own lives. Jesus said that we should first take the plank out of our own eye, then we will see clearly to remove the speck from our brothers eye (Matthew 7:5 NIV).

As new Christians, we are often impatient for others to change quickly, but we must remember to be as patient with others, as God is with us. When we focus on cleaning up our own lives, then we will be able to show others an example of what it is to live a godly life.

Let your light so shine before men,
that they may see your good works,
and glorify your Father which is in heaven.
Matthew 5:16 (NIV)

This doesn't mean that we can never offer helpful advice to a loved one, but we must allow the Holy Spirit lead us as to when and how.

It is very easy to find fault in other people, but it is not our place to bring judgment upon them. Remember to walk in mercy just as God is merciful with you. God is the only judge, be careful to not put yourself in His place!

Do not judge, or you too will be judged.
Matthew 7:1 (NIV)

Prayer

Lord, please help me not to focus on what I think needs to be changed in the lives of others, but on what needs to be changed in my own life. I desire to be a good example of how to live the life You've given to me. Forgive me for judging others, and continue to teach me to walk in Your mercy. In Jesus' Name I pray, Amen.

Reflection

Have I been focused on changing others, rather than changing myself?

Scripture Reading

Matthew 7 & Galatians 6:1-6

Day 72

Sick Puppies

As a dog returns to its vomit, so a fool repeats his folly.
Proverbs 26:11 (NIV)

We cannot continue repeating our same foolish mistakes and expect things in our lives to be different. We must learn from our mistakes and use the wisdom that God has given us, to make choices that will bless our future.

God will warn us when we are headed in the wrong direction. His Holy Spirit that lives within us, will reveal the truth when we are about to make a bad decision. But, it is left for us to make the right choice.

Wise people see danger
and go to a safe place.
But childish people keep on going
and suffer for it.

Proverbs 27:13 (NIrV)

Now is a good time for us to grow up and take responsibility for our lives. It is time for us to choose wisdom. God will honor and bless us for making good choices.

Those who do what is wrong
really earn nothing,
but those who do what is right
will certainly be rewarded.
Proverbs 11:18 (NIrV)

Prayer

Father God, thank You for giving me the wisdom that will help me avoid repeating past mistakes. Please help me to always take heed when the Holy Spirit warns me not to make a bad decision. In Jesus' Name I pray, Amen.

Reflection

Have I been stuck in a pattern of repeating my past mistakes?
If so, how can I break this pattern to bring positive change in my life?

Scripture Reading

Proverbs 9 & Proverbs 4:18

In God We Trust

*Trust in the Lord with all your heart,
and lean not on your own understanding;
He shall direct your paths.
Proverbs 3:5-6 (NKJV)*

We really can trust God with our lives. We do not understand all of His ways, but we know His heart. He is always there to guide, guard, and protect us. If we will honor Him in everything we do, He will make our paths smooth and straight.

Now, this does not mean we will never have problems or run into obstacles, but He will give us the power to overcome them, causing us to become stronger with each battle.

We are able to live in perfect peace, knowing that no matter what comes our way, God is on our side.

*And the peace of God,
which transcends all understanding,
will guard your hearts and your minds in
Christ Jesus. Philippians 4:7 (NIV)*

Through Jesus, who lives in each of us, we have victory in every situation!

*That's because everyone
who is a child of God
has won the battle over the world.
Our faith has won the battle for us.
1 John 5:4 (NIrV)*

Prayer

Heavenly Father, I know You are always there to guide, guard, and protect me. Please show me how to have more faith and trust in You, so I can receive Your perfect peace that surpasses all understanding. In Jesus' Name I pray, Amen.

Reflection

Have I made a conscious decision to put all of my trust in God, concerning my life?

Scripture Reading

Philippians 4 & Romans 1:17

A Party in My Mouth

Lord, I will give you honor.
You brought me out of deep trouble.
You didn't give my enemies the joy of seeing me die.
Lord my God, I called out to You for help
and You healed me."
Psalm 30:1-2 (NIrV))

God has literally saved us from death: physical, emotional, and spiritual. We have reason for His praises to continually be on our lips! He deserves all our thanks, all our praise, and a life lived to honor Him.

You turned my loud crying into dancing.
You removed my black clothes and dressed me with joy.
So my heart will sing to you.
I can't keep silent.
Lord, my God, I will give you thanks forever.
Psalm 30:11-12 (NIV)

Now, that is how we should live the rest of our lives: In constant praise and thanksgiving, honoring and serving Him!

As we continue to praise Him and give Him thanks for all He has done for us, this releases Him to bless us even more! Our life can become a never-ending cycle of praising the Lord, and Him turning our praise back into blessing for our lives. What an awesome way to live!

Prayer

Wonderful Lord! Thank You for saving my life from death and destruction. Your praise will be forever on my lips. I will take joy in forever singing Your praises! In Jesus' Name I pray, Amen.

Reflection

What are some things I can begin to praise and thank God for right now?

Scripture Reading

Psalm 135 & Psalm 136

I've Got You. Love, God

'The mountains might shake.
The hills might be removed.
But my faithful love for you will never be shaken.
And my covenant that promises peace to you
will never be broken, says the Lord.
He shows you His loving concern.'
Isaiah 54:10 (NIrV)

The whole world around us might be in trouble, financially as well as spiritually, but God will make sure we are protected in the midst of it all.

A thousand may fall at your side,
ten thousand at your right hand,
but it will not come near you.
You will only observe with your eyes
and see the punishment of the wicked.
Psalm 91:7-8 (NIrV)

We are God's children and He has promised to keep us safe in a world that is filled with evil.

The Lord is faithful.
He will strengthen you.
He will guard you from the evil one.
2 Thessalonians 3:3 (NIrV)

We are called to pray for the rest of the world, during this time of extreme darkness and sin, that they will come out of the darkness into the light. As we pray for others who are in worse situations than ours, we will be able to get our minds and our focus off our own fears.

Darkness covers the earth
and thick darkness is over the peoples,
but the Lord rises upon you
and His glory appears over you.
Nations will come to your light,
and kings to the brightness of your dawn.
Isaiah 60:2-3 (NIV)

Prayer

Dear God, Thank You for being my safety and refuge, during these evil and uncertain times. Please teach me how to pray for others during this time of extreme darkness, so they too may come into Your Light. In Jesus' Name I pray, Amen.

Reflection

Have I been spending time in prayer for other people to come out of the darkness of the world, into the Light of God?

Scripture Reading

Psalm 27 & Isaiah 54:14

Go Fish

"Come follow me,' Jesus said,
'and I will make you fishers of men.'
Matthew 4:19 (NIV)

We have all been given the wonderful gift of our salvation, and freedom from addiction. It is now our newfound, joyous responsibility to share this amazing gift of freedom with the rest of the world, who are lost.

…Freely you have received, so freely give.
Matthew 10:8 (NIV)

We must take what we have learned and share it with the addicts who are still suffering, as well as others who do not know Jesus!

People desperately need to hear the truth of the gospel of Jesus Christ. They need to hear how He can set them free from addiction, and any other type of bondage in their lives.

You will open eyes that can't see.
You will set the prisoners free.
Those who sit in darkness will come out of
their cells.
Isaiah 42:7 (NIrV)

We do need to be careful how, when, and where to witness to other addicts. It may not be wise, in every situation, to go back around people who are in their active addiction. The Holy Spirit will guide you when you are strong enough to do that. It may be safer at times, to pray for some people from a distance, until we are built up strong and secure in the Lord. It would also be wise to have a "prayer partner" with you, in any unsure situation.

Jesus wants to use each of us to bring His love and His message to a world that is filled with pain and suffering. He will take all the pain and suffering of our past, and now use it for the good of others, as they see Jesus glorified in us.

Prayer

Jesus, please help me be a witness to others about You, and the freedom and joy You can bring into a lost and hurting life. I ask that You give me wisdom on how, when, and where it is safe to carry this message. In Jesus' Name I pray, Amen.

Reflection

With whom can I share the truth of Jesus and the freedom only He can bring?

Scripture Reading

Deuteronomy 6 & Mark 16:15

Day 77

Priceless Thoughts

*Your eyes saw my body before it was formed.
You planned out how many days I would live.
You wrote down the number of them in Your book
before I had lived through even one of them.
Psalm 139:16 (NIrV)*

God loves you so much! He wants you to have the fulfillment of all His blessings and promises in your life. He loved you even before you were knit together in your mother's womb. He made a beautiful plan for your life, in advance. He thinks about you all the time and wants a close relationship with you.

*God, Your thoughts about me are priceless.
No one can possibly count them all up.
Psalm 139:17 (NIrV)*

You are very special and precious to God. He created you because He longs to have relationship with you; He wanted you to be a part of His eternal family.

*He will take great delight in you,
He will quiet you with his love,
He will rejoice over you with singing.
Zephaniah 3:17*

Can you imagine? The most high God, Creator of Heaven and Earth, the One who holds the stars in His hand and calls forth the wind and rain, *jubulantly sings* over you! That is an amazing serenade!

God also created us to have the freedom of choice. He gives His love freely and does not force us to love Him back. He wants us to *choose* to love and honor Him. Will you sing a love song back to Him?

When we make the quality decision to respond to His love, by living in obedience, loving Him, and walking in close relationship with Him, He is then able to bless our lives abundantly.

Prayer

Dear God, Your love for me is amazing and Your thoughts toward me are priceless. I want to honor You in everything I do. Thank You for all of my many blessings. In Jesus' Name I pray, Amen.

Reflection

Take some time now, and let yourself soak in the knowledge of how much God loves you and desires to have a relationship with you.

Scripture Reading

Psalm 84 & Psalm 5:12

My Walk

_____

_____

_____

_____

_____

_____

_____

_____

_____

_____

_____

_____

_____

My Walk

_____

_____

_____

_____

_____

_____

_____

_____

_____

_____

_____

_____

_____

Daily Decrees

1. I can always depend on God and His Word to never change.

2. In God, I find my stability, strength, and hope.

3. In God, I can find joy, even in difficult situations.

4. I am blessed, for my eyes see, and my ears hear God.

5. I will always seek God first in times of trouble.

6. I will seek counsel only from God and godly people.

7. Lord, I believe!

8. I will do all of my work as unto the Lord.

9. Because I love the Lord, I will not sin!

10. I will repent, turn away from all my sin, and live a pure and holy life.

Stability

Jesus Christ is the same yesterday and today and forever.
Hebrews 13:8 (NIrV)

We will always be able to depend on Jesus Christ and His Word to never change. Jesus and His Word always was, always is, and always will be final authority over everything that is in existence.

Heaven and earth may pass away,
but my words will never pass away.
Luke 21:33 (NIV)

The Word of the Lord is our flawless authority and guide for life.

All scripture is given by inspiration of God,
and is profitable for doctrine, for reproof, for correction,
for instruction in righteousness.
2 Timothy 3:16

The Bible is also our deed to inheritance. As God's children, we are also His heirs. Ephesians tells us that because of Jesus, everything in Heaven is available to us! We can access our inheritance because we are now part of God's household. The Bible is the family guide, explaining how to live as sons and daughters in our new home, the Kingdom of God.

I pray also that the eyes of your heart
may be enlightened
in order that you may know the hope
to which he has called you,
the riches of his glorious inheritance
in the saints
and his incomparably great power
for those of us who believe.
Ephesians 1:18-19

If we will learn to always lean upon Jesus and His Word for our direction in life, and obey Him, we will always find stability, hope, and strength.

Prayer

Dear Jesus, I thank You that You are the same yesterday, today, and forever-- and so is Your Word. Help me to always lean on You and Your Word to find my stability, strength and hope. In Your Name I pray, Amen.

Reflection

Have I been depending on Jesus and His Word to find my stability, strength and hope?

Scripture Reading

Ephesians 1 & Isaiah 40:8

Joyous Obstacles

Consider it pure joy, my brothers,
whenever you face trials of many kinds,
because you know that the testing of our faith develops perseverance.
James 1:2-3 (NIV)

As Christians, we will still have problems in life to face.

In this world you will have trouble.
But take heart! I have overcome the world.
John 16:22

There will be trials we must face. But we don't face trouble like the rest of the world does; we know the One who has overcome the world and He lives in us! Jesus has made us overcomers with Him. Trouble gives us opportunity to practice our faith and know the joy that comes with victory.

Many things that we go through, work strength in us that has eternal value. We don't always understand everything, but some things are for certain: God is Good and He will not leave you. Continue to submit your life to Him. Don't doubt who He is or what He says, just because a circumstance doesn't feel good. Ask Him for wisdom and understanding - ask Him for the keys to overcome. You are created to win! When we are in a difficult situation and are unsure of what to do, all we have to do is take it to God in prayer.

If any of you lack wisdom,
he should ask God,
who gives generously to all
without finding fault,
and it will be given to him.
James 1:5 (NIV)

Our relationship with Jesus gets closer and closer, because we experience His faithfulness. Our trust grows, as we allow our understanding to increase in the midst of trouble. This is why we can still have joy in the midst of trials and tribulation. With faith, we will overcome each challenge!

Prayer

Father, help me to remember that You are always there to help me through all my difficult situations. Thank You that I can find joy in a bad situation, knowing it will make me stronger. In Jesus' Name I pray, Amen.

Reflection
What are some of the obstacles facing me?
How can I find joy in each of these situations?

Scripture Reading
2 Corinthians 4 & Psalm 121:1-2

Day 80

Hearing God

*But blessed are your eyes for they see
and your ears for they hear.*
Matthew 13:16 (NKJV)

God speaks to us in many different ways. You may hear a voice speaking on the inside and instinctively know it is God. Sometimes you may simply have thoughts, and feel God's Spirit on them. Other times, you might "see" things in the spirit, meaning you may have a picture, image, or a complete vision in your mind's eye. You then need to pray for God to help you understand what it means. Some people have open visions from God that they actually see with their human eyes. God has even been known to speak audibly to people. But most of the time, it is through a still, small voice on the inside of us.

The closer we are in relationship with God, the more our spiritual senses will be in tune with what He is revealing to us. God wants to speak to us in many ways and on many levels. We just need to position ourselves to hear from Him. "Positioning yourself" means seeking Him in prayer, and in the Word, and also quieting yourself to listen for His voice.

The Lord will tell you how much He loves you, the future He has planned for you, assignments He has for you, changes He wants to help you with, as well as how He would like you to pray for others and yourself. These are just a few of the things the Lord may talk to you about. The list goes on and on...there is always something new and wonderful with God!

Sin in our lives will actually dull our spiritual senses and can cause us to be misguided in hearing the Lord. Sin is not worth cutting off the voice of God in our lives. Being in close communion with Him is more important than anything!

*For this people's heart has become calloused;
they hardly hear with their ears, and they
have closed their eyes. Otherwise they might
see with their eyes, hear with their ears, understand with their hearts and turn,
and I would heal them.*
Matthew 13:15 (NIV)

Prayer

Lord, please awaken all of my spiritual senses. I want to be able to hear, see, or feel what You are saying, or trying to show me. Sharpen any of my senses that have become dull because of sin. I want to hear what You are saying to me, clearly. In Jesus' Name I pray, Amen.

Reflection
Have I been paying attention to my spiritual senses?
What are some of the ways God has used to speak to me?

Scripture Reading
Matthew 13 & Isaiah 30:21

Wise Counsel

*Make sure no one captures you. They will try to capture you
by using false reasoning that has no meaning.
Their ideas depend on human teachings.
They also depend on the basic things
the people of this world believe.
They don't depend on Christ.
Colossians 2:8 (NIrV)*

We have to be very careful about who we receive counsel from. We can't expect to get good, godly advice from people who do not know the Lord.

That does not mean we should look down on people who are not Christians, but we do have to be careful on what we receive from them, because their values are not based on the principles of God. Always go first to the Lord with your problems to seek His wisdom.

*I will instruct you
and teach you in the way you should go;
I will counsel you and watch over you.
Psalm 32:8 (NIV)*

Sometimes we think that we have good counsel when I find someone who agrees with what I want to do. Godly counsel will never go against what God says in His word. There are times when we may want something so much that we have blinders on, making it hard to know the right decision. Wise counselors will not just tell you what you want to hear, they will hear God's heart for you.

God will help you find good Christian people that you may go to, if you need someone to talk with. Look for people who show that they have the fruit of the Spirit operating in their lives: love, joy, peace, patience, kindness, goodness, faithfulness, and self control. But no matter what, always make sure God is the one you go to, when making a final decision.

Prayer

Father God, I know You are always there to counsel me in times of confusion or uncertainty. I trust that You will put godly people in my life that I can talk to in times of need. Please give me wisdom in choosing people I can trust, to give me sound and wise advice. In Jesus' Name I pray, Amen.

Reflection
Have I been seeking counsel from the right people?

Scripture Reading
Colossians 2 & Proverbs 12:26

Lord, I Believe

*Immediately, the father of the child cried out
and said with tears,
'Lord, I believe; help my unbelief!'
Mark 9:24 (NKJV)*

I have learned to use this short prayer over and over again, each time I have a doubtful thought. "Father, I <u>do</u> believe. Please help my unbelief!"

When we are experiencing doubt, we can go to Jesus and ask Him to increase our faith. The Bible says that every man is given a measure of faith to build upon (Romans 12:3). Sometimes, when we become discouraged, it causes us to have unbelief in situations, but we must continue to trust God to come through for us, even if circumstances do not look good at the time.

*Let not your heart be troubled.
Trust in God; trust also in me.
John 14:1*

We build up our faith by spending time with the Lord in prayer, reading His word, and hearing what He says to us. As human beings, we will experience times of doubt or unbelief. During these times press into the word and ask Jesus to help you develop your faith so you will be able to overcome in "impossible" situations.

*Let us fix our eyes on Jesus,
the author and perfector of our faith,
who for the joy set before Him
endured the cross scorning its shame,
and sat down at the right hand of the throne
of God.
Hebrews 12:2 (NIV)*

Prayer

Lord, I <u>do believe</u>! Please help my unbelief! In Jesus' Name I pray, Amen.

Reflection

Where have I allowed discouragement to cause unbelief in difficult situations?

Scripture Reading

Matthew 9 & Matthew 17:10

Day 83

I'm Not Working for the Man

*Whatever you do, work at it with all our heart,
as working for the Lord, not for men,
since you know that you will receive an inheritance
from the Lord as a reward.
Colossians 3:23 (NKJV)*

In everything we do, whether it is service/volunteer work, work for the ministry, or our job in the world, we are to do our work as unto the Lord. If we do our work in honor of God, He will surely bless us. So, let's do every job to the best of our ability and use every gift the Lord has given us to be a blessing to our employers, and others in our work!

*It is the Lord Christ you are serving.
Colossians 3:23 (NIV)*

Not all jobs will be easy and not all people will be easy to work with, but when we work as unto the Lord, we can find joy in any task.

In everything we do, let's let people see the light of God and His good qualities shining out of us. We have to remember that as God's children, we are out there representing God and our brothers and sisters in Christ.

*Let your light so shine before men,
that they may see your good works,
and glorify your Father which is in heaven.
Matthew 5:16*

Prayer

Dear God, please help me to do all my work as unto You, so that people who see my good work, may give You the glory. In Jesus' Name I pray, Amen.

Reflection

Have I been working as unto the Lord?
How can I begin honoring the Lord more in my work?

Scripture Reading

Psalm 100 & Deuteronomy 10:12

Licensed to Sin?

What shall we say then?
Shall we continue in sin that grace may abound?
Certainly not!
How shall we who died to sin live any longer in it?
Romans 6:1-2 (NKJV)

Grace is not a license to sin. Just because God forgives us of all our sin, does not mean we should take this for granted and continue to live with sin in our lives.

When we made the decision to turn our will and our lives over to God, by asking Jesus to come into our hearts, we died to sin and we were born to righteousness. The definition of righteousness is to live in a way that is morally right. We are new creations in Christ. The old is gone and the new has come (2 Corinthians 5:17)!

We are called to be set apart from the world, to do great works in God's name that will lead others to Christ. We cannot set a good example when we are living in sin. But ultimately, sin destroys our most precious gift—our relationship with the Lord! God has made us His friend, let's be a good friend to Him.

Nobody is perfect. No man is totally without sin. But, there is a big difference between making a mistake one time and repeating the same sin over and over again, asking for forgiveness. If we do that, our heart is not truly repentant. True repentance is followed by change. God has given us all the power we need, to turn from sin and live in a way that is godly and pure.

For sin shall not be your master,
because you are not under law,
but under grace. Romans 6:14 (NIV)

Prayer

Father, please forgive me of all my sins and for any time I've repeated the same sins instead of having true repentance. Please help me to turn away from all sin in my life and follow with godly change. In Jesus' Name, Amen.

Reflection

Is my heart been truly repentant and ready to walk out my righteousness in Christ?

Scripture Reading

Revelation 3 & Psalm 103:12

My Walk

My Walk

_____

_____

_____

_____

_____

_____

_____

_____

_____

_____

_____

_____

_____

Daily Decrees

1. I have been given the keys to the Kingdom of God!

2. I have God given authority in prayer.

3. I will never be vengeful to those who hurt me.

4. I will stay prepared against attacks from the enemy!

5. God is my top priority.

6. I love the Lord with all my heart, with all my mind, and with all my strength.

7. I will love my neighbor as myself.

8. I will learn to recognize the strategies of the enemy.

9. I do not war against flesh and blood, but against principalities.

10. Jesus is my solid foundation!

Powerful Keys

I will give you the keys of the kingdom of heaven,
and whatever you bind on earth will be bound in heaven, and whatever you loose on earth
will be loosed in heaven.
Matthew 16:19 (NKJV)

We are given authority from God, to use the power of binding and loosing in our prayers. One definition of bind is *to tie together, to strengthen and secure.* So, for example, we can bind our mind to the mind of Christ and His thoughts. We can also bind ourselves to God's will and purposes for our lives.

Another definition for bind is to be *constricting or restricting.* Using this context, we can bind the power of the devil in our lives or the lives of our loved ones, so he won't be able to operate freely and cause more damage. We might say, "Satan I bind you from operating in the life of my loved one!"

We have also been given the power and authority to loose. A definition of loose is *to free oneself by force* or *to shake off restraint.* Using this meaning, we can pray to loose the power of the enemy in our lives.

We can also pray to loose old, negative mindsets, thinking patterns, desires, and beliefs in our loved ones and ourselves.

Another definition of loose is *to release.* We can loose (or release) in prayer good things: joy, peace, blessings, freedom, and more!

Binding and loosing are very powerful and effective tools to use in prayer. They are keys, from the Kingdom of Heaven, to use in releasing Kingdom power in our lives.

Prayer

Dear God, I thank You that whatever I bind on earth is bound in Heaven and whatever I loose on earth is loosed in Heaven. Please give me wisdom in using the power of binding and loosing in my prayers. In Jesus' Name I pray, Amen.

Reflection

What are some things I can begin "binding" and "loosing" in my life
and the lives of my loved ones?

Scripture Reading

Proverbs 18 & Mark 11:23

Vengeance

Do not take revenge, my friends,
but leave room for God's wrath,
for it is written:
'It is mine to avenge; I will repay,'
says the Lord.
Romans 12:19 (NIV)

The Lord instructs us not to try to get even, or get back at someone for something they have done to hurt or offend us. This type of behavior is a trap from the enemy, which will keep us enslaved to bitterness and unforgiveness.

God sees and knows *everything* that happens on earth. He loves justice and will make things right. The Lord will take care of everything and everyone in His own way and in His own time.

Not only are we not to take revenge, but we are also instructed to be kind to those who mistreat us.

Love your enemies, do good to them,
and lend without expecting
to get anything back.
Then your reward will be great,
and you will be sons of the Most High,
because He is kind
to the ungrateful and wicked.
Luke 6:35 (NIV)

Of course, this does not give anyone license to abuse us. It just means we are not to treat others unkindly because they were unkind to us. I have personally found it to be very freeing to do good for the people who have hurt me. When we show someone love, even when they haven't done anything to deserve it, it often frees them to become a better person as well.

Love is a much more powerful weapon than hate. After all, Jesus overcame all of sin and death, and restored us to life through love.

Prayer

Father God, I repent for all of the times I have done things with revenge as my motive. Please give me the strength to be kind to people when they have treated me badly, and to offer forgiveness as freely as You have given it to me. In Jesus' Name I pray , Amen.

Reflection
What has been my attitude toward the people who have hurt me?

Scripture Reading
Proverbs 25 & James 1:19-20

Be Prepared

*The thief does not come except to steal, kill and to destroy.
I have come that they might have life,
and that they might have it more abundantly.
John 10:10 (NKJV)*

The enemy had an evil plan in our addiction. He wanted to take everything we had, destroy us, and ultimately take us out. But praise the Lord, by the grace of God we lived through it and God is here to bring restoration to our lives so we may now live life to its fullest!

God will give us all the strength and resources we need to rebuild our lives, but the battle is not over. The enemy is mad about our recovery and he still has plans to steal, kill, and destroy. The good news is, as long as we remain in Christ Jesus, the enemy's plans will not succeed.

There is a wonderful purpose and plan for your life. You can't afford to believe differently. The enemy knows your potential and wants to rob you of what is rightfully yours. Believe what God says about you and don't let anyone or anything convince you otherwise.

We must stay on our guard. We cannot afford to become negligent in building our relationship with God. Without Him, we are nothing, but with Him we can stand up against *anything* that comes our way. The enemy doesn't stand a chance! If God is for us, who could be against us (Rom. 8:31)?

*The eternal God is your refuge,
and underneath are the everlasting arms.
He will drive out your enemy before you,
saying 'Destroy him!'
Deuteronomy 33:27 (NIV)*

Prayer

Oh Lord, thank You that the enemy has not, and will not succeed in his plans to destroy me! Thank You for protecting my life. Please teach me how to stay prepared against all attacks from the enemy on my life. In Jesus' Name I pray, Amen.

Reflection

Have I been doing what I need to do spiritually,
to stay prepared against attacks from the enemy?

Scripture Reading

Psalm 18 & Ephesians 3:16-17

The Greatest Commandment

Love the Lord your God
with all your heart and with all your soul
and with all your mind and with all your strength.
Mark 12:30 (NIV)

It is vital that God come first in your life and that He is your top priority. Place God before your other relationships, jobs, recreation—put God before everything else in your life! Our God is jealous, when we give more of our heart, time and attention to things other than Him.

> *For the Lord your God is*
> *a consuming fire,*
> *a jealous God.*
> *Deuteronomy 4:24 (NIV)*

We love God because He first loved us (1John 4:19). Our love is a response to His lavish, overwhelming, everlasting love. He loved you from the beginning of time and looked ahead, eagerly, for the day you would be born. He was so excited for your arival!

The world doesn't teach this kind of love. God's love is never withdrawn from us. He is never in a bad mood. He always wants to be with us and share who He is.

When we experience this kind of love, we can't help but respond with wanting more and more of His goodness. In the light of His love, everything else feels dull. We will want to spend more time in His presence and in His Word than we do in all the things of the world. We will also honor Him by obeying all of His commandments. In His love, we gain *everything*.

While we don't love Him just to receive blessing, when we choose to love and honor Him in all our ways, it frees Him to bless our lives in a mighty way.

Prayer

Dear God, I love You with all my heart, with all my mind, and with all my strength. Please reveal to me if there is anything in my life that I am putting before You, so I can get my priorities in order. I want to always put You first in my life. In Jesus' Name I pray, Amen.

Reflection
Is God first in my life? Are there other things I have been giving too much time to?

Scripture Reading
Deuteronomy 11 & Joshua 22:5

The Second Greatest Command

…Love your neighbor as yourself…

Mark 12:31 (NIV)

We learned yesterday that the greatest commandment is to love God with all our heart, soul, mind, and strength. The next verse says that the second greatest commandment is to love our neighbor as we love ourselves. Who is our neighbor? It is whoever is in front of us at any given time. We are to walk in love with everyone, at all times.

It's true that some people are easier to love than others, but our job is to love them, not to judge them. We do not get to pick and choose whom we love. Love is not optional – it is the *only* option.

When we have experienced this amazing love of God and we've spent time with Him as He pours out His love on us, we will be able to love others too! When we are filled up with God's love, it will flow out of us. It becomes easier to love my neighbor, when I know how much I am loved.

So, not only do I love the Lord, because He first loved me; I also love *you* because He first loved me.

Focus on your neigbor's strengths and good qualities rather than their faults and weaknesses. We will run into love tests with some people along the way but, with God's help, we can use them as stepping-stones that will help build our love and character. In this way, they become a blessing to us!

It is impossible to have truly unconditional love for others without experiencing God's unconditional love ourselves. So, when you run into a "love test," open your heart for the love that Jesus lavishes on you, and you will have more than enough for your neighbor.

Prayer

Dear God, I really do want to love others as I love myself. Please teach me how to love everyone, even when it is not easy and give me the strength to pass each love test. In Jesus' Name I pray, Amen.

Reflection
How can I love others as myself?

Scripture Reading
1 John 4 & John 13:34-35

War!

*For we do not wrestle against flesh and blood,
but against principalities, against powers,
against the rulers of the darkness of this age,
against spiritual hosts of wickedness in the heavenly places.*
Ephesians 6:12 (NKJV)

There are battles of spiritual warfare going on around us at all times. Good against evil, and light against darkness. We must learn to recognize strategies of the enemy in our lives, so we can pray against them. We need to understand that people are not our real opponents, but the evil spirits that are operating through them are.

The devil knows all about our past and what our wounds and weaknesses are. Therefore, he knows what buttons we have that can be pushed and he will use people to do it. He will especially use people who do not know the Lord, but at times he may even use Christians.

When things start going wrong left and right, when people seem to be picking fights with us for no reason, or we start to feel a lot of unusual sickness, pressure, oppression, or depression, it is likely an attack of the enemy. The good news is that with Jesus, who lives inside of us, we have all the power we need to stand against anything that comes against us.

*You, dear children, are from God
and have overcome them,
because the one who is in you
is greater than the one who is in the world.*
1 John 4:4 (NIV)

This verse says we have the power and authority to overcome evil spirits because of the power and authority of Christ, who is in each of us!

When we feel like we are under spiritual attack, we are to call upon the name of the Lord and take authority over any attack of the enemy, in the Name of Jesus. No weapon formed against us will prosper! As long as we stay strong in the Lord, the enemy cannot prevail over us.

Prayer

Dear God, I thank You for the power of Jesus Christ in me that has authority over all the power of the enemy. Please teach me how to pray against all spiritual attacks. I know that in You, no weapon formed against me will prosper. In Jesus' Name I pray, Amen.

Reflection
Have I been battling against flesh and blood rather than against principalities?
Scripture Reading
Psalm 138 & Romans 8:38-39

Our Rock

Therefore whoever hears these sayings of mine, and does them, I will liken him to a wise man who built his house upon the rock.
Matthew 7:24 (NKJV)

When we make the choice to use Jesus and His Word as the foundation that we build our lives upon, then our "Spiritual House" will be able to stand strong against the storms of life. Our foundation will be solid!

However, if we do not choose to build our lives upon the principles of God, our "Spiritual House" will be weak and the storms of life will cause us to fall.

But here is what happens when people
listen to my words and do not obey them.
They are like someone who builds a house on soft ground instead of solid rock.
The moment the river rushes against that house, it falls down.
It is completely destroyed.
Luke 6:49 (NIrV)

Wisdom would say to us that it is much better to be safe in the arms of the Lord, to stand against such storms with Him as our solid foundation. Jesus is our rock! When we build on Him *nothing* can shake us!

The Lord is the one who keeps you safe.
So let the Most High God be like a home to you.
Then no harm will come to you.
No terrible plague will come near your tent.
Psalm 91:9-10 (NIrV)

Praise the Lord! Now *that* is security! In this book, I have given you an excellent foundation of scriptures to build your "Spiritual House" upon. Now it is up to you! I encourage you to hold on to this book and look back upon the scriptures, as needed. You will also want to refer back to the writing you have done, to see how far the Lord has brought you.

Remember to stay in the Word of God and in constant communion with Him. That is the *only* way for us to *walk it out* and live our lives in true freedom. God bless you!

Prayer

Jesus, I choose to build my life with You and Your Word, as my solid foundation, so I may stand strong in the face of life's storms. In Your Wonderful Name I pray, Amen.

My Walk

_____

_____

_____

_____

_____

_____

_____

_____

_____

_____

_____

_____

_____

My Walk

_____

_____

_____

_____

_____

_____

_____

_____

_____

_____

_____

_____

_____

_____

My Walk

_____

_____

_____

_____

_____

_____

_____

_____

_____

_____

_____

_____

_____

My Walk

_____

_____

_____

_____

_____

_____

_____

_____

_____

_____

_____

_____

_____

_____

_____

Additional copies of this book
and other book titles from
Walk It Out Ministries
are available at **Walkitoutministries.com**

BULK ORDERS:

We have bulk/wholesale prices for stores and
ministries. Please contact:
ginger@walkitoutministries.com

Made in the USA
Columbia, SC
07 June 2021